# PRESIDENT'S MALARIA INITIATIVE

# Zimbabwe

# Malaria Operational Plan FY 2016

# TABLE OF CONTENTS

# ABBREVIATIONS and ACRONYMS

| | |
|---|---|
| ACT | Artemisinin-based combination therapy |
| ANC | Antenatal care |
| AS/AQ | Artesunate-amodiaquine |
| ASL | Above sea level |
| BCC | Behavior change communication |
| CDC | Centers for Disease Control and Prevention |
| DEHO | District Environmental Health Officer |
| DHIS2 | District Health Information System 2 |
| DHS | Demographic and Health Survey |
| DMO | District Medical Officer |
| DPS | Directorate of Pharmacy Services |
| EHT | Environmental health technician |
| EUV | End-use verification |
| FETP | Field Epidemiology Training Program |
| FY | Fiscal year |
| GHI | Global Health Initiative |
| Global Fund | Global Fund to Fight AIDS, Tuberculosis and Malaria |
| HMIS | Health Management Information System |
| iCCM | Integrated community case management |
| IEC | Information, education and communication |
| IPTp | Intermittent preventive treatment for pregnant women |
| IRS | Indoor residual spraying |
| ITN | Insecticide-treated mosquito net |
| LLIN | Long-lasting insecticide-treated net |
| LMIS | Logistics Management Information System |
| LT | Light trap |
| M&E | Monitoring and evaluation |
| MIP | Malaria in pregnancy |
| MIS | Malaria indicator survey |
| MMCM | Malaria community case management |
| MOHCC | Ministry of Health and Child Care |
| MOP | Malaria Operational Plan |
| NIHR | National Institute of Health Research |
| NMCP | National Malaria Control Program |
| NMSP | National Malaria Strategic Plan |
| OP | Organophosphates |
| OR | Operational Research |
| PCU | Program Coordinating Unit |
| PMI | President's Malaria Initiative |
| RDNS | Rapid Disease Notification System |

| | |
|---|---|
| RBM | Roll Back Malaria |
| RDT | Rapid diagnostic test |
| SHC | School health coordinator |
| SP | Sulfadoxine-pyrimethamine |
| UNICEF | United Nations Children's Fund |
| USAID | United States Agency for International Development |
| USG | United States Government |
| VHW | Village health worker |
| WHO | World Health Organization |
| WHT | Ward Health Team |
| ZIPS | Zimbabwe Integrated Push System |
| ZAPS | Zimbabwe Assisted Pull System |

# I. EXECUTIVE SUMMARY

When it was launched in 2005, the goal of the President's Malaria Initiative (PMI) was to reduce malaria-related mortality by 50% across 15 high-burden countries in sub-Saharan Africa through a rapid scale-up of four proven and highly effective malaria prevention and treatment measures: insecticide-treated mosquito nets (ITNs); indoor residual spraying (IRS); accurate diagnosis and prompt treatment with artemisinin-based combination therapies (ACTs); and intermittent preventive treatment of pregnant women (IPTp). With the passage of the Tom Lantos and Henry J. Hyde Global Leadership against HIV/AIDS, Tuberculosis, and Malaria Act in 2008, PMI developed a U.S. Government Malaria Strategy for 2009–2014. This strategy included a long-term vision for malaria control in which sustained high coverage with malaria prevention and treatment interventions would progressively lead to malaria-free zones in Africa, with the ultimate goal of worldwide malaria eradication by 2040-2050. Consistent with this strategy and the increase in annual appropriations supporting PMI, four new sub-Saharan African countries and one regional program in the Greater Mekong Subregion of Southeast Asia were added in 2011. The contributions of PMI, together with those of other partners, have led to dramatic improvements in the coverage of malaria control interventions in PMI-supported countries, and all 15 original countries have documented substantial declines in all-cause mortality rates among children less than five years of age.

In 2015, PMI launched the next six-year strategy, setting forth a bold and ambitious goal and objectives. The PMI Strategy 2015–2020 takes into account the progress over the past decade and the new challenges that have arisen. Malaria prevention and control remains a major U.S. foreign assistance objective and PMI's Strategy fully aligns with the U.S. Government's vision of ending preventable child and maternal deaths and ending extreme poverty. It is also in line with the goals articulated in the RBM Partnership's second generation global malaria action plan, *Action and Investment to defeat Malaria (AIM) 2016-2030: for a Malaria-Free World* and WHO's updated *Global Technical Strategy: 2016-2030*. Under the PMI Strategy 2015–2020, the U.S. Government's goal is to work with PMI-supported countries and partners to further reduce malaria deaths and substantially decrease malaria morbidity, towards the long-term goal of elimination.

Zimbabwe was selected as a PMI focus country in FY 2011.

This FY 2016 Malaria Operational Plan presents a detailed implementation plan for Zimbabwe, based on the strategies of PMI and the National Malaria Control Program (NMCP). It was developed in consultation with the NMCP and with the participation of national and international partners involved in malaria prevention and control in the country. The activities that PMI is proposing to support fit in well with the National Malaria Strategic Plan (NMSP) and build on investments made by PMI and other partners to improve and expand malaria-related services, including the Global Fund to Fight AIDS, Tuberculosis, and Malaria (Global Fund) malaria grants. This document briefly reviews the current status of malaria control policies and interventions in Zimbabwe, describes progress to date, identifies challenges and unmet needs to achieving the targets of the NMCP and PMI, and provides a description of activities that are planned with FY 2016 funding.

The proposed FY 2016 PMI budget for Zimbabwe is $14.5 million. PMI will support the following intervention areas with these funds:

**Insecticide-treated nets (ITNs)**: PMI is supporting the Ministry of Health and Child Care's (MOHCC) goal of universal coverage with 340,000 (2015) and 919,976 (2016) long lasting insecticide-treated nets (LLINs) in 47 districts with moderate to high transmission of malaria. With FY 2015 and 2016 funds, PMI will support free, routine LLINs distribution through antenatal care (ANC) and immunization clinics to pregnant women, and children under one year of age, respectively, and through school and community programs.

**Indoor residual spraying (IRS)**: Zimbabwe has a long history of IRS dating back to the 1950s. The NMCP IRS strategy focuses on 47 high-burden malaria districts throughout the country. With FY 2015 and FY 2016 funds, PMI will provide comprehensive support of four high burden districts (Mutare, Chimanimani, Nyanga, and Mutasa) of Manicaland Province (a province that contributes about 51% of malaria cases in Zimbabwe) using organophosphate (OP) insecticides, covering approximately 163,922 structures, and protecting approximately 350,000 people in the targeted IRS districts. PMI will also work with NMCP and its partners to expand support for entomological monitoring to assure quality spraying, careful vector monitoring and developments in insecticide effectiveness and resistance.

**Malaria in pregnancy (MIP)**: Zimbabwe's MIP policy focuses on high-burden malaria districts, and advocates for directly observed administration of three doses of sulfadoxine-pyrimethamine (SP) during scheduled ANC visits. With FY 2016 funds PMI will procure approximately 161,000 treatments of SP for distribution to health facilities located in the target districts for IPTp. Funding will also be used to improve quantification of antimalarial drugs including SP in an effort to minimize stock outs. In addition, PMI support will promote ITN use, early ANC visits and prompt malaria case management for pregnant women. Lastly, PMI and partners will work with the NMCP to introduce the newly approved WHO SP policy in Zimbabwe, which recommends giving IPTp at each scheduled antenatal care visit at least one month apart starting at the beginning of the second trimester.

**Case management**: Since 2007, the first-line treatment for malaria has been the artemisinin based combination (ACT) drug artemether-lumefantrine (AL). The NMCP policy requires that, where possible, all suspect cases of malaria undergo diagnostic confirmation by microscopy or a rapid diagnostic test (RDT). At the end of 2010, the pharmacy board and the laboratory regulatory council changed the policy to allow community-based health workers (CHWs) to perform diagnosis using RDTs and dispense ACTs for positive cases. Historically, CHWs have included village health workers (VHWs) and school health masters (SHMs). VHWs are trained in integrated community case management (iCCM) as well as more comprehensive malaria community case management (MCCM) to deliver integrated care. SHMs used to teach about

6

malaria prevention and dispensed chloroquine to school children but have not been a functional group for case management in the past five years, while VHWs remain an active group. The NMCP has discussed plans to revive the SHMs to diagnose and dispense ACTs and are currently managing distribution of LLINs through schools. In addition to supporting the drug management and distribution systems (Zimbabwe Informed Push System [ZIPS] and Zimbabwe Assisted Push System [ZAPS]), with FY 2016 funds PMI will procure approximately 1.87 million RDTs, approximately 500,000 treatments of AL, 20,000 treatments of ASAQ, 10,000 artesunate suppositories and 166,000 vials of artesunate injectable for treatment of uncomplicated and severe malaria. The support will include updating worker guidance materials and training of health workers and VHWs and providing monitoring and supervision.

**Health systems strengthening/capacity building**: PMI will support capacity building by contributing to the Field Epidemiology and Laboratory Training Program (FELTP), to promote malaria-specific field studies and support at least two trainees to enhance field epidemiology skills. This activity will strengthen mid- to high-level capacity, and develop skilled field supervisors in the malaria field as they learn how to actively identify, evaluate, and help scale up effective activities against malaria. With FY 2016 funds PMI will also continue to build university laboratory capacity for both epidemiologic and entomologic surveillance sample analysis. This activity will increase access to quality analysis for malaria surveillance activities in Zimbabwe, while also building human capacity and improving local platforms for teaching critical laboratory skills.

**Behavior change communication (BCC)**: The NMSP objectives form the basis for the implementation of the BCC activities for malaria control program in Zimbabwe. To achieve NMSP's desired outcome, PMI supports BCC activities that aim to promote correct and consistent use of ITNs, acceptance of IRS, adherence to diagnosis and treatment, and uptake of MIP. With FY 2016 funds PMI will support VHWs, school, and community leaders to conduct interpersonal communication on key malaria messages around LLINs, malaria in pregnancy, RDTs, and ACTs in the 47 districts with the highest malaria transmission. These activities will be complemented by printed materials that accompany packaged messages on LLINs, RDTs and ACTs; radio spots; and drama skits at various locations including religious institutions, schools, and community events. The primary focus for all activities will be to support LLIN distribution (routine and campaign), improve MIP uptake (SP at each ANC at least one month apart, starting in the second trimester, use of LLINs during pregnancy, and early and effective diagnosis and treatment of malaria), and promote IRS and appropriate case management. Recommendations from the BCC assessment to be conducted in November 2015 will provide guidance for improving PMI support in these primary focus areas.

**Monitoring and evaluation (M&E)**: The National Malaria M&E Strategy and Plan developed in 2008 was extended in 2014 to 2017, in line with the WHO pre-elimination strategies. It describes, by program area, the type of data needed, the indicators, data collection and flow, analysis, reporting, feedback and stakeholders' responsibilities.  With FY 2016 funding, PMI will continue to support malaria surveillance and national survey activities, M&E trainings at all levels including VHWs, as well as supervisory and district health facility trainings. In addition, PMI support will facilitate quarterly meetings for district-, provincial- and national-level representatives to meet and discuss surveillance and M&E related issues. PMI plans to support the Malaria Indicator Survey in 2016, and because of the intense resources required for this endeavor, NMCP has delayed the next therapeutic efficacy study until 2017. PMI will continue supporting LLIN durability monitoring, following LLINs that will be disseminated through school-based distribution in September 2015.

**Operations research (OR):** Zimbabwe is still early in the development of an operational research (OR) portfolio. However some priority areas have been identified and include: 1) malaria in mobile and remote populations; 2) role of community health workers in malaria pre-elimination; and 3) documenting progress towards pre-elimination. In FY 2016, PMI will support two operational research activities. The first will evaluate the effectiveness of VHWs in decreasing the malaria morbidity and mortality burden through active or reactive case detection. The second activity will assess the presence of outdoor feeding malaria vectors and asses human nighttime activities, including outdoor-sleeping, that might increase exposure to malaria infection.

## II. STRATEGY

### 1. Introduction

When it was launched in 2005, the goal of PMI was to reduce malaria-related mortality by 50% across 15 high-burden countries in sub-Saharan Africa through a rapid scale-up of four proven and highly effective malaria prevention and treatment measures: insecticide-treated mosquito nets (ITNs); indoor residual spraying (IRS); accurate diagnosis and prompt treatment with artemisinin-based combination therapies (ACTs); and intermittent preventive treatment of pregnant women (IPTp). With the passage of the Tom Lantos and Henry J. Hyde Global Leadership against HIV/AIDS, Tuberculosis, and Malaria Act in 2008, PMI developed a U.S. Government Malaria Strategy for 2009–2014. This strategy included a long-term vision for malaria control in which sustained high coverage with malaria prevention and treatment interventions would progressively lead to malaria-free zones in Africa, with the ultimate goal of worldwide malaria eradication by 2040-2050. Consistent with this strategy and the increase in annual appropriations supporting PMI, four new sub-Saharan African countries and one regional program in the Greater Mekong Subregion of Southeast Asia were added in 2011. The contributions of PMI, together with those of other partners, have led to dramatic improvements in the coverage of malaria control interventions in PMI-supported countries, and all 15 original countries have documented substantial declines in all-cause mortality rates among children less than five years of age.

In 2015, PMI launched the next six-year strategy, setting forth a bold and ambitious goal and objectives. This PMI Strategy 2015-2020 takes into account the progress over the past decade and the new challenges that have arisen. Malaria prevention and control remains a major U.S. foreign assistance objective and PMI's Strategy fully aligns with the U.S. Government's vision of ending preventable child and maternal deaths and ending extreme poverty. It is also in line with the goals articulated in the RBM Partnership's second generation global malaria action plan, *Action and Investment to Defeat Malaria (AIM) 2016-2030: For a Malaria Free World,* and WHO's updated *Global Technical Strategy:2016-2030.* Under the PMI Strategy 2015-2020, the U.S. Government's goal is to work with PMI-supported countries and partners to further reduce malaria deaths and substantially decrease malaria morbidity, towards the long-term goal of elimination.

Zimbabwe was selected as a PMI focus country in FY 2011.

PMI invested malaria resources in Zimbabwe to fill important gaps in funding and technical guidance. The primary donors to Zimbabwe's malaria control effort are the Global Fund, PMI, and the Government of Zimbabwe (GoZ) – each historically contributing 64%, 28%, and 7% respectively to the total malaria budget between 2008 and 2012.

This fiscal year (FY) 2016 Malaria Operational Plan presents a detailed implementation plan for Zimbabwe, based on the strategies of PMI and the Zimbabwean National Malaria Control Program (NMCP). It was developed in consultation with the NMCP and with the participation of national and international partners involved in malaria prevention and control in the country. The activities that PMI is proposing to support fit in well with the national malaria control strategy and plan and build on investments made by PMI and other partners to improve and expand malaria-related services, including the Global Fund to Fight AIDS, Tuberculosis, and Malaria (Global Fund) malaria grants. This document briefly reviews the current status of malaria control policies and interventions in Zimbabwe, describes progress to date, identifies challenges and unmet needs to achieving the targets of the NMCP and PMI, and provides a description of activities that are planned with FY 2016 funding.

## 2. Malaria situation in Zimbabwe

Zimbabwe has seasonal and geographic variation in malaria transmission that corresponds closely with the country's rainfall pattern. In general, the major malaria transmission season occurs during the rainy season between November and April, with the average temperature ranging between 18 and 30 degrees Celsius. Peak transmission season is February through April. The annual rainfall varies from less than 700 mm in Matabeleland Province to more than 1,500 mm in Manicaland Province. Malaria transmission is lower in the low rainfall areas and higher in the high rainfall provinces.

Geographically, Zimbabwe is divided by a central watershed lying higher than 1,200 meters above sea level and flanked north and south by low lying areas. In 1986, the country was divided into three malaria epidemiological areas based on altitude above sea level (ASL). The three epidemiological zones in terms of malaria transmission are: areas below 900 meters ASL in the north, and below 600 meters ASL in the southern regions, where malaria was considered to be perennial. Areas between 900-1200 meters ASL north and 600-900 meters ASL south were where malaria is seasonal and prone to epidemics. In areas above 1,200 meters ASL north and 900 meters ASL south malaria transmission does not normally occur. Traditionally, higher areas have been described as unstable, and lower areas as stable.

Zimbabwe is divided into ten provinces (two of which are urban), 63 rural districts, and 1,200 wards. Forty-seven of the rural districts are considered malarious and of those, 30 are considered high malaria burden districts.

**Table 1: Zimbabwe Malarious Districts by Province**

| Province | # Malarious Districts |
|---|---|
| Mashonaland East | 5 districts |
| Mashonaland West | 7 districts |
| Mashonaland Central | 8 districts |
| Manicaland | 7 districts |
| Matabeleland South | 5 districts |
| Midlands | 4 districts |
| Matabeleland North | 6 districts |
| Masvingo | 5 districts |
| **TOTAL** | **47 districts** |

Population estimates for Zimbabwe vary due to recent migration within and outside the country. The 2015 population estimate, as projected from the 2012 census, is 13.5 million and it is estimated that about half of this population lives in malaria risk areas.

*Plasmodium falciparum* accounts for more than 98% of all reported malaria cases; *P. ovale* and *P. malariae* account for the remainder. The Centers for Disease Control and Prevention (CDC) light traps and pyrethrum spray catches conducted at PMI-supported sentinel sites in 2013-14 showed the major malaria vector to be *Anopheles (An.) gambiae s.l.* in most parts of the country in line with findings from previous vector distribution studies. Contrastingly, *An. funestus* was the predominant vector in Mutasa and Mutare districts of Manicaland Province. There is geographic variation in malaria burden risk across and within provinces. Figure 1 shows a comparison of the burden of malaria by district for 2014.

**Figure 1: Annual Malaria Incidence Rates by District, 2014, Zimbabwe**

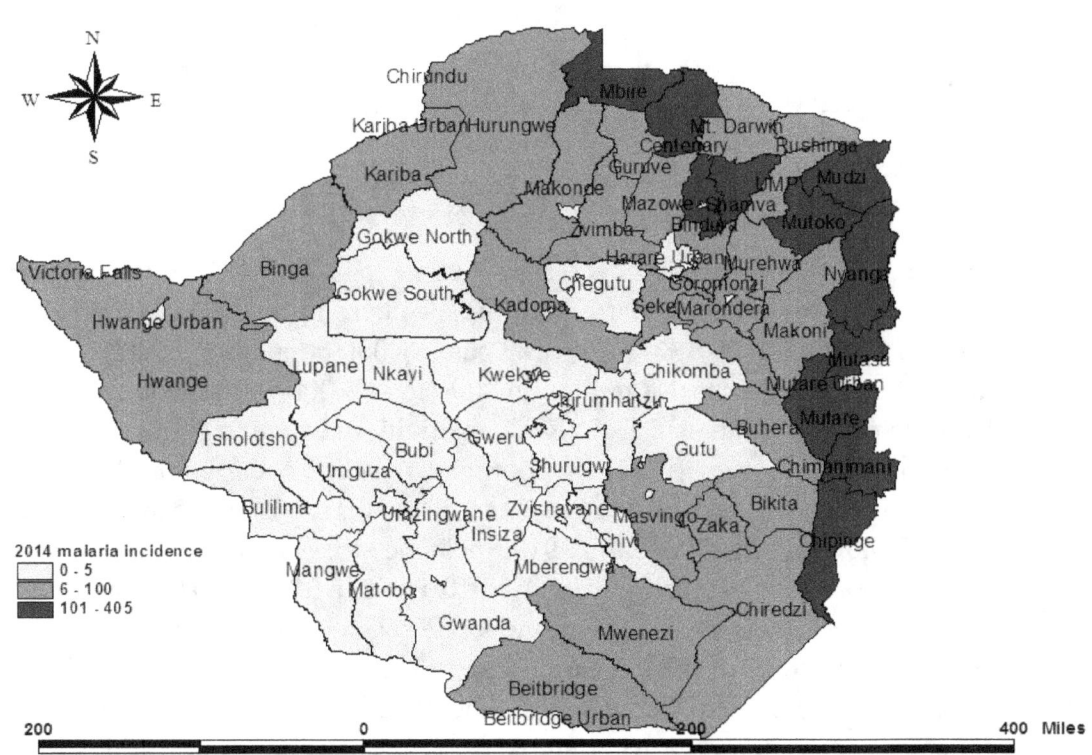

According to Zimbabwe District Health Information System 2 (DHIS2) data, approximately 83% of all malaria cases and 50% of all malaria deaths in 2014 originated from three eastern rural provinces: Manicaland, Mashonaland East and Mashonaland Central, with 42% of all cases and 26% of all deaths coming from Manicaland (Tables 2 and 3). This trend where the three provinces

11

rank highest in reported cases and deaths continues from 2013.

**Table 2: DHIS2 Malaria Morbidity data, 2014, Zimbabwe**

| Province | Malaria Cases* | % Contribution |
|---|---|---|
| Manicaland | 224,742 | 42.0 |
| Mashonaland Central | 130,211 | 24.3 |
| Mashonaland East | 88,773 | 16.6 |
| Subtotal (3 provinces) | 443,726 | 82.9 |
| Other Provinces | 92,057 | 17.2 |
| National | 535,783 | 100** |

*Diagnostically confirmed
** Exceeds 100% due to rounding

**Table 3: DHIS2 Malaria Mortality data, 2014, Zimbabwe**

| Province | Malaria Deaths | % Contribution |
|---|---|---|
| Manicaland | 184 | 25.8 |
| Mashonaland Central | 109 | 15.3 |
| Mashonaland East | 62 | 8.7 |
| Subtotal (3 provinces) | 355 | 49.8 |
| Other Provinces | 358 | 50.2 |
| National | 713 | 100 |

Overall, malaria incidence in Zimbabwe has decreased over the past decade. However, it remains a major challenge in certain provinces, districts, and wards. According to the NMCP's latest figures, malaria incidence decreased by 86% from 153 cases/1,000 population in 2004 to 22/1,000 in 2012. Reported cases decreased from 1.8 million in 2006 to 480,000 in 2014. National malaria prevalence is 0.4% slide positivity rate and 1.0% RDT positivity rate among children aged 6-59 months (2012 Malaria Indicator Survey [MIS]). A continuous decline occurred until 2012, but an upsurge in cases and incidence was recorded in 2013 and 2014 (Figure 2). Incidence declined by 86% from 2004 to 2012; however, from 2012 to 2013, incidence rose 32% from 22/1,000 to 29/1,000. The following year the rate increased again to 40/1,000, a 38% change from 2013. Most positive cases occurred in districts or areas of high-moderate seasonal malaria transmission. While it is acknowledged that some of the increase is due to increased diagnostic capacity, there may be other reasons that are unknown. Consequently, there are many activities, including operational research activities, planned to better understand the potential causes for this increase in incidence.

**Figure 2. Malaria Incidence Rates by Year, Zimbabwe, 2004-2014**

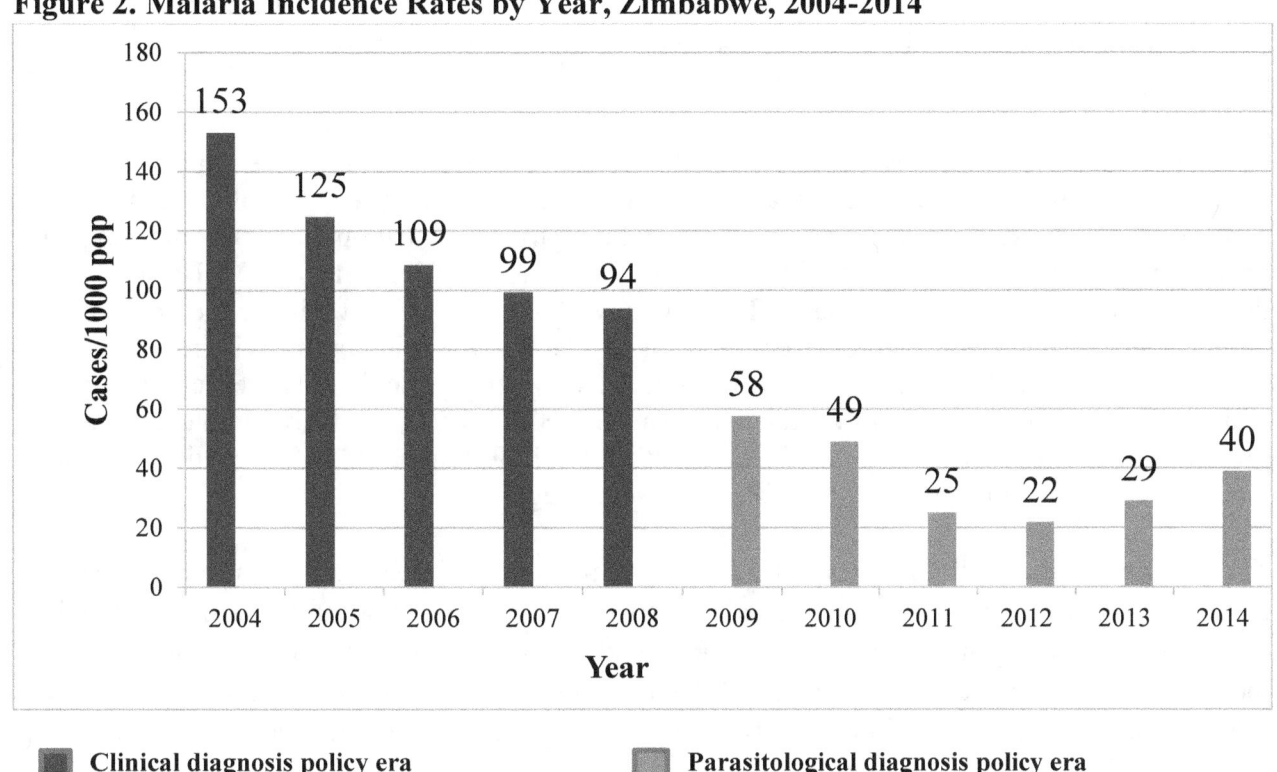

Source: Zimbabwe Health Information System

It is difficult to determine how much of the reduction in incidence from 2003 is due to migration, changing weather patterns, oscillations in data quality, or if this represents a true reduction due to effective malaria control interventions. The NMCP and World Health Organization (WHO) collaborated on a rapid impact assessment exercise in 2013 to determine the impact of the scaled up interventions on transmission trends, as well as on disease burden and mortality. They concluded that the decline in malaria inpatient admissions and deaths was seen after the shift in first-line treatment from choloroquine to its combination with SP, and the introduction of ITNs. In addition, a more dramatic decline resulted after the mass distribution of long-lasting insecticide-treated nets (LLINs) to the general population, as well as the introduction of ACTs in the public sector in 2008. Declines in malaria admissions and deaths were much greater in high transmission areas rather than in the low transmission areas. In-patient malaria cases decreased between 2013 and 2014. However, in-patient deaths showed no change.

3. **Country health system delivery structure and Ministry of Health and Child Care (MOHCC) organization**

The Ministry of Health and Child Care (MOHCC) has three main divisions: Policy Planning, Monitoring, and Evaluation; Curative Services; and Preventive Services, plus the Provincial Medical Directorates. The NMCP is under the Preventive Services directorate and is led by a director, supported by a team of senior officers responsible for: case management, monitoring and evaluation (M&E), vector control, behavioral change communication (BCC), and finance and administration.

At the provincial level, the Provincial Medical Director is responsible for all health activities, including malaria control, and has a team of managers responsible for epidemiology and disease control, nursing services, environmental health, administration, nutrition, health promotion and pharmacy. The Provincial Epidemiology and Disease Control Officers (PEDCO) also serve as the provincial focal person for malaria. The structure at the district level mirrors the province with a District Health Management Team (DHMT). The DHMT is led by the District Medical Officer (DMO), who is responsible for all health delivery services in the district including malaria. The DHMT works with ward health teams (WHTs) to coordinate and implement health programs. The District Environmental Health Officer (DEHO) manages IRS activities whereas the District Nursing Officer is responsible for case management related issues.

The primary health facility level is staffed by two–three nurses, one to two environmental health technicians (EHTs), and nurse aides. There are approximately 1,500 primary health facilities in Zimbabwe and each primary health facility is linked to a WHT comprised of community members such as village health workers (VHWs), school health teachers, headmen, chiefs, and religious leaders. The health facility staff is responsible for overseeing program implementation at ward level in conjunction with the WHT. The WHT members are volunteers, although trained community-based health volunteers receive an incentive of $14/month from the Global Fund grant for health system strengthening as well as the Health Transition Fund. An additional $1/month per VHW goes to the Department of Nursing in the MOHCC to support the VHW program.

The NMCP collaborates with diverse partners and has linkages with the following parastatal, governmental, and nongovernmental organizations:

1. National Institute for Health Research (NIHR), a government entity which operates a center for research, training, and service in the fields of disease control, biomedicine, and public health;

2. Nat Pharm, a parastatal organization which is responsible for the procurement, storage and distribution of all health pharmaceutical commodities, including malaria medicines;

3. Medicine Control Authority of Zimbabwe, a statutory government institution which is responsible for registration of all medicines in the country;

4. National Microbiology Reference Laboratory, a government entity which is responsible for internal quality assurance; and

5. Zimbabwe National Quality Assurance Program, a nongovernmental organization responsible for external quality assurance for laboratories.

The NMCP has ten national level staff in Harare and eight Provincial Malaria Focal Persons. In addition, there is one national level post, Chief Field Officer, supporting vector control as well as a Master of Public Health (MPH) student attached to the NMCP. At the national level, the NMCP develops policy, national guidelines, and training materials. The national level also oversees program implementation, M&E, resource mobilization and partnership coordination.

Due to Zimbabwe's economic collapse in 2008-09, all of the NMCP positions in Harare are supported by the Global Fund. The position of the Provincial Malaria Focal Person is also supported by the Global Fund while the other workers receive allowances from the Zimbabwe Health Worker Retention Scheme. A Malaria Logistics Focal Person who is funded by PMI sits at the MOHCC under the pharmacy directorate and spearheads malaria supply chain activities at MOHCC headquarters and coordinates with the NMCP. The GoZ budget is planned annually, based upon district annual plans which are consolidated at the provincial and later at the national levels.

In addition to the above financial assistance, other local and international non-governmental organizations (NGOs) support malaria control activities.

## 4. National malaria control strategy

The vision of the NMCP's 2008-2015 extended National Malaria Strategic Plan (NMSP) is a malaria-free Zimbabwe with the goal to "reduce malaria incidence from 95/1,000 in 2007 to 10/1,000 by 2015 and reduce malaria deaths to near zero by 2015." The NMSP has been extended to 2017 and the stated goal is now: "To reduce malaria incidence from 22/1,000 persons in 2012 to 10/1,000 persons by 2017 and malaria deaths to near zero by 2017."

The key approaches of the NMSP include:
1. Universal access to malaria prevention and personal protection with: 90% of the population at risk covered by IRS and ITNs, and 85% coverage of monthly recommended dose of intermittent preventive treatment for pregnant women (IPTp2) attending antenatal care in medium-high transmission areas
2. Improve diagnosis and treatment of both uncomplicated and severe malaria
3. Improve detection and timely control of malaria epidemics, by detecting at least 100% of malaria epidemics within two weeks of onset
4. Expand districts implementing pre-elimination activities
5. Increase utilization of correct malaria prevention and control measures to at least 80% of the population at risk
6. Strengthen monitoring and improve evaluation of malaria activities at all levels
7. Expand and maintain strong multi-sectoral partnerships for effective program management and coordination.

## 5. Updates in the strategy section

In 2014, NMCP changed its policy from IPTp with two doses of sulfadoxine-pyrimethamine (SP) being given during pregnancy, and adopted the 2013 WHO recommendations for IPTp which does not state a maximum number of doses be given to all women regardless of the number of ANC visits. The policy is to give a pregnant woman a dose at every antenatal care (ANC) visit, as long as they are at least four weeks apart. The first dose is to be given at the beginning of the second trimester, and dosing continues up to the time of delivery. The WHO recommends women have at least four ANC visits during pregnancy.

The Global Fund invoked the Additional Safeguards Policy (ASP) in 2008 following the sequestration of Global Fund funds by the Reserve Bank of Zimbabwe. This meant that the Global Fund reserved the right to select the principal recipient (PR) for Global Fund grants, and it imposed stricter risk mitigation controls. Therefore since August 2009, the United Nations Development Program (UNDP) has been the PR for Global Fund grants in Zimbabwe.

After the review of the ASP in 2014, the Global Fund concluded that a national institution could be selected for programmatic PR-ship for malaria and tuberculosis (TB) and take over from UNDP. The Global Fund in consultation with the Country Coordinating Mechanism (CCM) then selected the MOHCC to be PR for TB and malaria during the implementation of the New Funding Model (NFM) 2015 - 2016. A Program Coordinating Unit (PCU) for Global Fund supported programs has been established to facilitate the smooth transitioning of the PR-ship from UNDP to MOHCC.

## 6. Integration, collaboration, and coordination

Both USAID and CDC support programs in three key areas of the U.S. Global Health Initiative (GHI): HIV/AIDS, TB, and malaria. With FY 2016 funding, PMI/Zimbabwe will actively seek opportunities to collaborate with other United States Government (USG) health programs so as to ensure maximum impact for every health dollar the USG invests in the country. Opportunities include the following:

*Maternal and child health services and malaria:* Since malaria prevention and control activities are implemented as part of integrated maternal and child health services, PMI will make a significant contribution to strengthening capacity to deliver these services. PMI will work with other USG-funded programs and other partners to support the comprehensive primary health care package, including the training and implementation of community-based diagnosis and treatment of fever, IPTp, and early treatment. PMI will continue to support universal coverage of LLINs via campaigns as well as the integration of LLIN distribution within routine ANC and expanded program on immunization (EPI) services.

*Integrated Community Case Management (iCCM):* With increasing numbers of home births, falling household compliance with key child health household practices, and added barriers to

16

care for women, newborns, and children (i.e., user fees and fewer rural health centers providing birthing and clinical care), the need is evident to focus increased attention on the community and households. PMI/Zimbabwe supports malaria prevention and treatment as a part of iCCM.

Beginning in early 2010, the MOHCC and its partners launched a training program to revitalize the VHW cadres. Other partners are also supporting iCCM. The United Nations Children's Fund (UNICEF) is currently supporting VHW training and providing other inputs such as bicycles, and the MOHCC is using Global Fund funding to expand VHW refresher training to all districts, provide VHW kits, and once again offer a monthly stipend (approximately $14 per month) to each VHW. The community-based maternal and newborn care manual, developed by WHO and UNICEF, comprises the primary content for the current VHW refresher training.

PMI has complemented other partner resources to integrate malaria community case management (MCCM) within the scope of the VHW program. PMI's partner is training VHWs to provide an integrated package of care using a revised community register as a job aid to record visits on conducting comprehensive care. Village health workers have an important role to play in mobilizing their communities, and identifying those women, infants, and sick children who require care, including those in hard-to-reach areas or groups.

*Strengthening of supply chain system:* PMI will also support the strengthening of supply chains, including support for the Zimbabwe Informed Push System (ZIPS) or its successor, Zimbabwe Assisted Pull System (ZAPS), which includes TB commodities, primary health care packages, and malaria commodities, namely rapid diagnostic tests (RDTs), SP, and ACTs.

*HIV/AIDS and malaria*: Based on a 2011 national survey the seroprevalence of HIV infections is high; an estimated 15.2% among individuals aged 15 to 49 years old are infected. Infection with HIV is higher among women (17.7%) than men (12.3%) and is modestly higher in urban areas (16.7%) than in rural (14.6%) areas. Areas where integration will be pursued between the MOHCC's HIV/AIDS Program and NMCP include: promoting adherence to universal precautions when taking blood samples, integrating laboratory quality assurance, providing LLINs to people living with HIV/AIDS, and ensuring appropriate malaria prevention services at Prevention of Mother-to-Child Transmission clinics. At the community level, PMI will support VHWs who provide RDT and ACT services to also communicate important messages regarding HIV prevention and testing.

*TB and Malaria:* The National TB Program supports the activities of village health promoters to inform and support TB diagnosis and follow-up. Where these promoters are the same cadres as the VHWs that provide RDT and ACT services, PMI will work to integrate activities across HIV, TB, and malaria.

*Routine partner collaboration and coordination:* Commitment to reducing the malaria burden and continuing on the path of malaria elimination is evident at the highest levels of the MOHCC.

The NMCP staff meets weekly to review work plans and monitor progress. The NMCP coordinates with partners through five malaria technical subcommittees: vector control, M&E, case management, BCC, and procurement and supply management. These subcommittees meet quarterly and are chaired by the NMCP or other MOHCC staff, and include the PMI/Zimbabwe in-country team and PMI implementing partners.

The NMCP participates actively in the multi-sectoral Inter Agency Coordination Committee on Health (IACCH) formerly "Health Cluster" group meetings, chaired by the MOHCC's Director of Epidemiology and Disease Control. The NMCP also participates in a number of sub-regional and cross-border initiatives, a priority for the program. The NMCP is an active partner of the RBM Southern Africa Regional Network (SARN) and with the Southern African Development Community (SADC) malaria network.

The NMCP is a member of the Malaria Elimination Eight (E8) countries comprised of four front line countries: Botswana, Namibia, South Africa, and Swaziland, and four second line countries: Angola, Mozambique, Zambia, and Zimbabwe. Inaugurated in 2009, the E8 countries have a collective goal to eliminate malaria in their region.

The program is also a member of the Trans-Zambezi Malaria Initiative (TZMI) with Zimbabwe, Zambia, Namibia, Botswana, and Angola. The TZMI is a convergence of five countries on the narrow Caprivi Strip with a total of 16 districts and a combined population of 1.5 million people at risk of malaria. Its vision is to eliminate malaria in the Trans-Zambezi communities with social and economic prosperity by 2020.

The Health Partners Development Group meets on a quarterly basis to discuss issues of mutual interest. Currently, USAID chairs these meetings with WHO being the alternate chair.

PMI, led by the PMI in-country team, will work closely with the NMCP, Roll Back Malaria (RBM) partners, Global Fund-funded, and other health-related programs in Zimbabwe to provide integrated services at the health facility and community level. PMI will work with others in USAID/Zimbabwe to ensure coordination of PMI-supported activities within the broader context of the health strategies. These approaches will ensure the most cost-effective implementation of prevention and treatment measures. PMI and NMCP have agreed on quarterly PMI implementing partners meetings, which include PMI Resident Advisors and Malaria Specialist, partners, and the NMCP.

In addition, PMI staff will provide leadership and technical assistance in other coordinating bodies such as the local RBM (including relevant RBM sub-committees). At the planning and implementation levels, PMI and other partners will work together to effectively fill commodity and human resource gaps.

### 7. PMI goal, objectives, strategic areas, and key indicators

Under PMI Strategy 2015-2020, the USG's goal is to work with PMI-supported countries and partners to further reduce malaria deaths and substantially decrease malaria morbidity, towards the long-term goal of elimination. Building upon the progress to date in PMI-supported countries, PMI will work with NMCPs and partners to accomplish the following objectives by 2020:

1. Reduce malaria mortality by one-third from 2015 levels in PMI-supported countries, achieving a greater than 80% reduction from PMI's original 2000 baseline levels.
2. Reduce malaria morbidity in PMI-supported countries by 40% from 2015 levels.
3. Assist at least five PMI-supported countries to meet the World Health Organization's (WHO) criteria for national or sub-national pre-elimination.

These objectives will be accomplished by emphasizing five core areas of strategic focus:

1. Achieving and sustaining scale of proven interventions
2. Adapting to changing epidemiology and incorporating new tools
3. Improving countries' capacity to collect and use information
4. Mitigating risk against the current malaria control gains
5. Building capacity and health systems towards full country ownership

To track progress toward achieving and sustaining scale of proven interventions (area of strategic focus #1), PMI will continue to track the key indicators recommended by the RBM Monitoring and Evaluation Reference Group (RBM MERG) as listed below:

- Proportion of households with at least one ITN
- Proportion of households with at least one ITN for every two people
- Proportion of children under five years old who slept under an ITN the previous night
- Proportion of pregnant women who slept under an ITN the previous night
- Proportion of households in targeted districts protected by IRS
- Proportion of children under five years old with fever in the last two weeks for whom advice or treatment was sought
- Proportion of children under five with fever in the last two weeks who had a finger or heel stick
- Proportion receiving an ACT among children under five years old with fever in the last two weeks who received any antimalarial drugs
- Proportion of women who received two or more doses of IPTp for malaria during ANC visits during their last pregnancy

## 8. Progress on coverage/impact indicators

Progress on coverage/impact indicators to date are noted in Table 4 below.

**Table 4: Evolution of Key Malaria Indicators in Zimbabwe from 2005 to 2012**

| Indicator | 2005 DHS | 2009 MIMS | 2010 DHS | 2012 MIS* |
|---|---|---|---|---|
| % Households with at least one ITN | 9% | 27% | 29% | 46% |
| % Households with at least one ITN for every two people | - | | | |
| % Children under five who slept under an ITN the previous night | 3% | 17% | 10% | 57.9% |
| % Pregnant women who slept under an ITN the previous night | | | 10% | ** |
| Proportion of women of child-bearing age who slept under an ITN the previous night | | | | 44.6% |
| | | | | |
| % Households in targeted districts protected by IRS | 15.2% | | 17% | 48.6% |
| | | | | |
| % Children under five years old with fever in the last two weeks for whom advice or treatment was sought | | | | 100% |
| | | | | |
| % Children under five with fever in the last two weeks who had a finger or heel stick | | | 7.4% | |
| Proportion of children under five years old with fever in the last two weeks who received treatment with ACTs | 5% | 14% | 2% | |
| % Children receiving an ACT among children under five years old with fever in the last two weeks who received any antimalarial drugs | - | - | - | - |
| | | | | |
| % Women who received two or more doses of IPTp during their last pregnancy in the last two years | | | 7% | 35% |

*MIS was conducted in 51 malaria endemic districts of eight rural provinces
**Data were collected on net use by women of child-bearing age but not among pregnant women specifically
- Data not available

## 9. Challenges and opportunities

Current USG restrictions prohibiting funding directly to the GoZ or any institution affiliated with the GoZ make it challenging to implement NMCP-led activities in Zimbabwe. However, PMI works through partners that operate under the leadership of the NMCP, planning and working closely with NMCP staff throughout all activities. District health staff, including EHTs and health facility workers, are responsible for the implementation of malaria prevention and control activities in communities, including the training and supervision of VHWs. Because of current USG policy in Zimbabwe, PMI is unable to support government staff per diem or allowances for routine visits to the field, such as monitoring, which are critical for successful program implementation; there are seldom funds available for supervision from GoZ. Global Fund has funded government staff per diem for some activities in the past. Nevertheless, ensuring that monitoring visits occur and that staff are compensated is a particular challenge. PMI partners are sometimes able to support GoZ staff to participate in training, monitoring and supervision events/visits.

Entomological surveillance needs to be intensified and expanded nationally given the increasing vector resistance to pyrethroid insecticide being observed in the highest burden districts. *Anopheles funestus,* a species which is resistant to pyrethroids and sensitive to DDT and more expensive organophosphates (OPs) and noted in recent years, remains a challenge in Manicaland's high burden districts. There is therefore a growing need for a strong vector resistance management strategy. In 2014 PMI provided comprehensive IRS services, using OPs in four high-burden districts of Manicaland. PMI plans to continue with the same package of support in 2015 spraying season.

While Zimbabwe has made improvements in the use of parasitological diagnosis of cases to guide treatment, diagnostic capacity needs a strong quality assurance/quality control (QA/QC) system to maintain and advance gains made. Because of critical challenges in administration and management with a local designated partner, PMI was unable to fund a QA/QC program for diagnostics last year. However, PMI has prepared a description of detailed needs in this area (supervision, tools, job aids, etc.) and this challenge may soon be addressed through funding from other donors.

In response to recent NMCP adoption of the latest WHO-recommended guidelines for IPTp and use of ACTs and parenteral artemisinin products for the treatment of uncomplicated and severe malaria, PMI updated health worker guidance materials and trained the health workforce, in which there are training gaps, high turnover, and hiring freezes. These policy changes provide opportunities for Zimbabwe to align with international and regional policies and enhance case management. However, they will also result in increased complexity in the supply chain management system. PMI will continue supporting the MOHCC to carry out the semi-annual exercise to quantify the current and future needs for life-saving medicines and medical supplies in country.

As the national incidence of malaria has decreased over the past decade, provinces bordering Mozambique report the highest number of cases annually, while others within the country, especially in the southern region of the country, report pre-elimination-level incidence. Cross border malaria with migration of both Zimbabweans and Mozambicans through official and unofficial border posts, often during peak mosquito biting periods, and differing preventive and clinical service availability in contiguous areas in each country are suspected reasons for the high burden. For example, Manicaland Province on the Zimbabwe-Mozambique border represents 42% of all of Zimbabwe's malaria cases (see Table 2).

Zimbabwe's malaria burden may be highest in Manicaland, but districts along the southern border approaching pre-elimination (see Figure 3) also illustrate the need for cross-border collaboration as part of Zimbabwe's malaria control strategy. Future plans will require balancing resources and priorities to address the heterogeneous malaria epidemiology and disease burden patterns as the country works to achieve the goals in the revised strategic plan.

**Figure 3: Proposed pre-elimination districts from 7 to minimum of 20 by 2017**

In 2014, malaria outbreaks were reported in six of the eight rural provinces of Zimbabwe. The most affected provinces for the last three years were Manicaland, Mashonaland Central and Mashonaland East provinces in that order, which all border Mozambique. This recurring challenge highlights the precarious nature of the gains made in malaria control in Zimbabwe. Responses to these outbreaks have been characterized by late detection and ineffective or no response. Nevertheless, it is important to better understand the changing burden and risk of malaria in these provinces and to understand the driving forces behind the outbreaks. Availing resources for outbreak control and continual training on M&E and health information systems will improve the capacity for recognizing and responding to epidemics.

## Table 5: Distribution of malaria outbreaks, 2014, Zimbabwe

| Indicator | Manicaland | Mash Central | Mash East | Mash West | Masvingo | Mat North | Mat South | Midlands | Total |
|---|---|---|---|---|---|---|---|---|---|
| Number of outbreaks confirmed | 76 | 7 | 38 | 0 | 7 | 1 | 1 | 0 | 130 |
| Cases reported during outbreak | 99,033 | 15,865 | 36,055 | 0 | 25,255 | 29 | 612 | 0 | 176,849 |
| Deaths reported during outbreak | 155 | 6 | 39 | 0 | 35 | 3 | 0 | 0 | 238 |

## III. OPERATIONAL PLAN

Through PMI, the USG is committed to working closely with host governments and within existing national malaria control plans. Efforts are coordinated with other national and international partners, including the Global Fund to Fight AIDS, Tuberculosis and Malaria (Global Fund), RBM, and the non-governmental and private sectors, to ensure that investments are complementary and that RBM and Millennium Development Goals are achieved.

In Zimbabwe, PMI collaborates and coordinates with the NMCP and other partners based upon the NMCP's strategic goals and priorities. The level of support for each of the interventions takes into consideration the contributions from other donors such as the GoZ, the Global Fund, and other stakeholders to ensure priority interventions are scaled up to fill gaps, avoid duplication, and address regional variations in malaria epidemiology and progress to date.

PMI support covers all of Zimbabwe's highest malaria burden provinces, including Manicaland. Some PMI support also cover districts along the southern border with areas approaching pre-elimination where cross-border collaboration is a priority for Zimbabwe's malaria control strategy. The current plan will balance resources and priorities to address the heterogeneous malaria epidemiology and disease burdens patterns as the country works to achieve the goals in the revised strategic plan.

### 1. Insecticide-Treated Nets

*NMCP/PMI objectives*

Zimbabwe's NMSP proposes universal coverage in targeted districts with LLINs as one of the country's key priorities for vector control in combination with IRS and targeted larviciding. The stated goal of continued decreases in transmission, if sustained as in the past decade, will support a shift from control towards pre-elimination strategies in large parts of the country over the coming years. The NMCP has worked to increase coverage of LLINs over the past several years with mass campaigns and routine distribution channels.

NMCP's LLIN targeted districts are 47 out of a total of 62 districts (47 considered malarious). The NMCP defines universal coverage as one net for every two persons or one net per sleeping space. The NMCP intends to: 1) increase the proportion of the general population sleeping under an LLIN to 80%, and 2) increase the number of children under five and pregnant women sleeping under an LLIN to 85% by 2015. The 2012 MIS reported that 46.4% of households owned at least 1 LLIN and 58.9% slept under a net in the 30 LLIN-targeted districts at the time. The next MIS will be conducted in 2016 and will indicate whether LLIN ownership and use has increased.

Despite a long history of IRS, NMCP in Zimbabwe recognizes that LLINs are a primary vector control tool and is shifting their culture to deploy LLINs and IRS in a more balanced, practical way. This is important to use funds as efficiently as possible. The Zimbabwe NMCP's vector control policy is to deploy both LLINs and IRS in the 47 malarious districts (See Table 6) with a commitment to achieve and maintain complete vector control coverage of all wards in the 47 malarious disticts with LLINs or IRS – no overlap of either vector control measure. The policy describes that LLINs complement IRS and is an important vector control strategy in both low transmission areas (primarily through routine distribution) and moderate to high transmission areas (through both routine and campaign distribution). The NMCP supports a mixed model of LLIN campaign distribution that includes distribution through public health facilities, community-based fixed-point campaigns, and subsequent mop-up campaigns.

Before 2014, NMCP relied solely on distribution through mass campaigns (fixed point distribution followed by mop-up). However, in late 2014 NMCP, supported by PMI and partners, began an LLIN routine distribution system pilot in four districts in Mashonaland West and Mashonaland Central.

**Table 6: NMCP/Zimbabwe LLIN Strategic Objective**

| Strategic Objective | Low-to-no transmission 16 districts (including urban metropolitan areas), 49% of population | Moderate-to-high transmission 47 districts, 51% of population |
|---|---|---|
| **To ensure universal access of the population at risk to effective and appropriate malaria prevention interventions by 2017** | **Routine** LLIN in ANC, EPI, Elementary Schools, and Community (via VHWs)  **No mass** LLIN distribution  **No IRS** | **Routine** LLIN in ANC, EPI, Elementary Schools, and Community (via VHWs)  **Mass** LLIN distribution through campaigns  or  **IRS** in targeted wards of the 47 districts, based on previous transmission patterns and incidence data  ALL wards are covered by either blanket IRS or campaign LLINS. |

According to NMCP calculations using the NetCalc quantification tool, Zimbabwe has nearly achieved universal coverage, ~90%, an achievement which is included as a key component of the NMSP, guided by global guidance on strategies for effectively cutting transmission. The 2016 Malaria Indicator Survey will be an opportunity to survey LLIN coverage and use and provide more certainty to the NetCalc estimate. As outlined in Table 6 above, NMCP's strategy is to cover moderate to high transmission areas (47 districts, 51% of the population at risk) with IRS and to complement this strategy with periodic mass distribution of LLINs and routine distribution in between campaigns in 47 high transmission districts. Wards within the 47 malarious districts that do not benefit from IRS will receive nets via campaign and routine. Low-no transmission districts will receive nets through continuous routine distribution.

Given the scarcity of resources, the program will optimize targeted outlets by providing an opportunity for all Zimbabweans to have access to new and replacement LLINs routinely – for pregnant women, at ANC children under five at EPI, at third and sixth grade in elementary schools, and to all community members via VHW community networks.

PMI/Zimbabwe will continue working with NMCP to refine and distill a vector control policy that has already begun to take shape. These discussions will also include the value of creating a multi-year vector control strategy.

*Progress since PMI was launched*

From 2008 to 2010, a total of 1.9 million LLINs were distributed free to targeted communities. Global Fund Round 8 phase 1 procured 1,219,309 LLINs and UNITAID procured 640,557 LLINs in 2009. The LLINs distributed by 2010 are estimated to have covered 83% of the population in 30 targeted districts, assuming that one LLIN is shared between two people. These LLINs were distributed through mass campaigns using public health facilities as fixed distribution points. Before each distribution cycle, a registration/census was carried out to determine the number of individuals in the home, sleeping spaces, and to estimate nets required.

According to the 2010-2011 DHS, 29% of households owned at least one ITN and 10% of children under five and 10% of pregnant women slept under an ITN the previous night.

The 2012 MIS provides estimates of the progress made in coverage of preventive and treatment services for malaria. The MIS found that in the 30 LLIN target districts, 55.7% of households had at least one net. Among households with nets, 83.3% of them had at least one LLIN. The coverage increased substantially from the 2008 Multiple Indicator Monitoring Survey (MIMS) figures, where the proportion of households with at least one LLIN was only 36.9%.

A total of 3,201,573 LLINs was needed for mass distribution in 2013. Through the support from the Global Fund (1,368,279), PMI (699,500) and other partners, the country mobilized 2,067,779 LLINs which were distributed to the 34 priority districts. Districts were prioritized by highest transmission risk. After the distribution, a gap of 1,133,794 LLINs for 2,294,079 people in 13 eligible districts remained; this area was targeted for nets in 2014.

*Progress during the past 12 months*

In September/October 2014, PMI distributed 660,688 LLINs via campaign in the moderate to high malaria transmission districts including: Chiredzi, Chipinge, Gokwe, Makoni, Bulilima, Mangwe, Gwanda, Zvimba, Shamva Urban and Beitbridge Urban. In previous distributions public institutions such as boarding schools, orphanages and elder care homes were omitted. On top of the above mentioned districts, these institutions in the following districts were also covered: Mazoe, Centenary, Guruve, Rushinga, Lupane, Binga, Zaka, Masvingo, Kwekwe, Mberengwa, Gokwe North, Chimanimani, Mutare, Nyanga and Mutasa.

PMI continued to support the advent of the routine distribution pilot in four districts – Mt. Darwin, Mazowe, Hurungwe, and Makonde. The effort began in Mt. Darwin and then moved to Mazoe, Hurungwe, and Makonde. PMI partners worked with NMCP to supervise the pilot start-up and complete several rounds of supervisory visits which allowed for refinements in the program. The supervisory team looked at supply logistics, performance of LLIN-dispensing staff on the ground, interaction with beneficiaries, and documentation. At least 13 recommendations emerged from the joint supervision of the pilot and will be addressed in the next few months.

Mazowe is the pilot district selected for a baseline survey to determine changes before and after the pilot, including LLIN ownership and use. In addition a process evaluation for the pilot is scheduled for July 2015 which is designed to show progress achieved so far and help inform how to best manage scale-up of the pilot.

## Commodity gap analysis

**Table 7. ITN Gap Analysis**

| Calendar Year | 2015 | 2016 | 2017 |
|---|---|---|---|
| Total Targeted Population | 6,768,344 | 6,842,796 | 6,918,067 |
| **Continuous Distribution Needs** | | | |
| Channel #1: ANC | 270,734 | 273,712 | 276,723 |
| Channel #2: EPI | 223,355 | 225,812 | 228,296 |
| Channel #3: 3rd and 6th Graders | 249,424 | 837,357 | 837,357 |
| Channel #4: Community | 37,500 | 245,956 | 255,794 |
| *Estimated Total Need for Continuous* | 781,013 | 1,582,837 | 1,598,170 |
| **Mass Distribution Needs** | | | |
| 2016 mass distribution campaign | 0 | 2,069,127 | 0 |
| *Estimated Total Need for Campaigns* | 0 | 2,069,127 | 0 |
| **Total Calculated Need: Routine and Campaign** | **781,013** | **3,651,964** | **1,598,170** |
| **Partner Contributions** | | | |
| ITNs carried over from previous year | 199,753 | 0 | 0 |
| ITNs from MOH | 0 | 0 | 0 |
| ITNs from Global Fund Malaria Grant | 0 | 847,084 | 0 |
| ITNs from Other Donors | 0 | 0 | 0 |
| ITNs planned with PMI funding | 340,000 | 919,976 | 310,680 |
| Total ITNs Available | 539,753 | 1,767,060 | 310,680 |
| **Total ITN Surplus (Gap)** | (241,260) | (1,884,904) | (1,287,490) |

## Plans and justification

Additional resources will be needed for the period 2015 onwards as the country moves forward to expand the continuous distribution pilot to maintain the universal coverage. PMI will distribute 539,753 LLINs in the pilot during the remaining 2015 year. The NMCP is planning to conduct mass distributions of LLINs in 2016 in identified areas of need throughout the 47 targeted districts, as well as scale up routine distribution. The NMCP estimate of campaign need is 2,069,127 LLINs. Since some LLINs were distributed in 2014, a proportion of the LLINs in some of these 47 districts are assumed to be viable with a third year of protection. . However, since the previous campaigns were conducted in a staggered, piece-meal manner and not precisely recorded, NMCP has decided to include all LLIN-eligible areas in the 47 districts for the 2016 campaign.

PMI and Global Fund have committed 1,767,060 LLINs for 2016 but these do not meet the NMCP estimated need for the year (campaign and routine) of 3,651,964, leaving a significant gap of 1,884,904 LLINs for 2016. With such a large gap, NMCP and partners are not confident of being able to meet the total need in 2016 with current resources and will likely consider adding a second phase of distribution to the campaign distribution in 2017. NMCP will consider reprogramming Global Fund resources to purchase more LLINs. Because of the LLIN gap, the 2016 campaign and routine distribution efforts will need to prioritize LLINs to the most needy geographic areas and vulnerable populations, such as Manicaland, Mashonaland East, and Mashonaland Central with Zimbabwe's highest malaria burden during the campaign, and to pregnant women at routine distribution ANC outlets.

Major activities related to routine distribution in the coming years include:

1. PMI and NMCP discussions to continued refinement of the overall vector control policy in 2015 and 2016.
2. Development of routine distribution roll-out plan based on the process evaluation.
3. Production of the Mazowe district baseline report.
4. End-line results from the Mazowe district will be collected in November 2015.
5. Next routine school distribution and accompanying phase 1 of the net durability study is planned for September 2015. See M&E section for more information.
6. 2016 LLIN campaign.

The 2015 DHS and the 2016 MIS will provide an update of LLIN ownership and consistent use in malarious districts. MIS data will be used to more accurately understand coverage and use quantity and patterns which have been estimated with mathematical modeling since 2012.

*Proposed activities with FY 2016 funding: ($2,100,000)*

PMI will continue to fill strategic gaps in LLIN procurement not covered by the Global Fund and the GoZ. Using FY 2016 funding, PMI will support LLIN procurement and distribution for the ongoing continuous distribution approach designed to ensure high coverage of new cohorts of pregnant women and children, and to replace worn out LLINs distributed through previous campaigns to all Zimbabweans that need LLIN protection. Specific activities to be supported by PMI with FY 2016 funding include:

- *Procure LLINs for routine replacement and campaign distribution*: Procure approximately 919,976 LLINs (400,000 with MOP FY 2016 funds and an additional 519,000 LLINS with DELIVER pipeline savings) via campaign and routine distribution.

The routine distribution scale up will have started in 2015/2016 and will be further defined by the program evaluation report. It may include all four distribution channels – ANC, EPI, elementary schools (Grades 3 and 6), and community – in low-to-no transmission areas and high transmission areas though ANC will be prioritized. *($1,600,000)*

- *Planning, distribution, and monitoring of routine and campaign LLIN distribution*: PMI will provide support to the NMCP in logistics and operations to strengthen LLIN distribution systems including supply chain management to ensure continuous availability of LLINs and to strengthen the distribution systems capacity for efficient delivery of LLINs to end users. *($500,000)*

- *Technical assistance to implement LLIN activities*: One USAID technical assistance visit to support overall LLIN distributions *(included in core USAID Administration budget)*.


## 2. Indoor residual spraying

*NMCP/PMI objectives*

Zimbabwe has a long history of implementing IRS, dating back to 1949. Currently, the NMCP IRS strategy targets one round of spraying per year in each of the 47 malarious districts. There is not yet an articulated strategy on the combination or balance of IRS and LLINs. The NMCP aims to reduce the transmission of malaria by scaling up effective vector control interventions (IRS and LLINs) to 90% of the population at risk. According to the 2010-2011 DHS, 17% of households received IRS within the past 12 months. This figure ranged from 40% in higher-burden malaria provinces (Matabeleland North) to 2% in Harare, where there is little or no malaria transmission.

The 2012 MIS showed that 48.6% of households in the 47 targeted districts were sprayed within the past 12 months. This figure ranged from 65.6% in Mashonaland East to 36.3% in Mashonaland West.

The program used DDT until 1991, when it was replaced with pyrethroids. However, after the switch, a marked increase in reported malaria cases was observed, prompting the reintroduction of DDT in 2004. The IRS program continued with a mix of DDT and pyrethroids up to the 2013 spraying season. In 2014, entomological monitoring data showed a marked resistance to pyrethroids, particularly in Manicaland Province (See Table 8 below).

**Table 8: Insecticides Used in Resistance Testing in Zimbabwe, 2014**

| Province | Insecticides Used in Resistance Testing | | | | | |
|---|---|---|---|---|---|---|
| | Lambda - cyhalothrin (0.05%) | Deltamethrin (0.05%) | Bendiocarb (0.1%) | DDT (4%) | Pirimiphos - methyl (1.0%) | Etofenprox (0.5%) |
| Manicaland – Burma Valley | R | -- | R | S | S | R |
| Manicaland – Honde Valley | R | -- | R | – | S | R |
| Matabeleland North | R | -- | S | S | S | -- |
| Matabeleland South | R | -- | S | PR | S | S |
| Midlands | S | S | S | S | S | -- |
| Mashonaland Central | S | S | S | S | S | S |
| Masvingo | S | -- | S | S | S | S |
| Mashonaland East | S | S | -- | S | S | -- |
| Mashonaland West - Kasimure | R | -- | R | S | S | PR |
| Mashonaland West - Chakari | R | -- | -- | S | S | PR |

Note: S=susceptible; R=resistant; PR=potentially resistant

The WHO criteria for noting susceptibility to insecticide was used:

Susceptibility = Mortality rate of the exposed vector greater than or equal to 98 percent

Possible Resistance = Mortality rate of the exposed vector equal to or between 90 percent and 97 percent

Resistance = Mortality rate of the exposed vector is less than 90 percent.

Due to this resistance, the NMCP included IRS using organophosphates in Zimbabwe's concept note for the Global Fund New Funding Model (2015-16). In the 2014 spraying season (October to December), PMI supported the NMCP to spray IRS using organophosphates in four districts of the areas with highest pyrethroid resistance in Manicaland province. With anticipated Global Fund support, the NMCP intends to triple the number of districts being covered with organophosphates, with the goal of creating a protected barrier along the lengthy Zimbabwe-Mozambique border. Areas showing little to no pyrethroid resistance continued to be sprayed using a mix of pyrethroids and DDT.

Technical support and coordination for entomological monitoring in Zimbabwe is provided by the National Institute of Health Research (NIHR), formerly known as the "Blair Research Institute." During the early 1990s, vector mapping and vector bionomics were identified as priority activities along with insecticide susceptibility monitoring and bioassay assessments. A total of 16 entomological monitoring sites, 2 sites per province, were established with Global Fund support in 2010. While these sites do have some equipment and some staff have been trained, support is needed to ensure consistent entomological surveillance across all sites.

*Progress since PMI was launched*

Due to the NMCP's experience and capabilities to conduct IRS, from 2012–2013 PMI provided a limited package of IRS support, stressing environmental compliance, and contributing to planning meetings, trainings, monitoring and evaluation, operational logistics and some procurement of insecticides and equipment in pyrethroid districts. This enabled PMI to fill the operational gaps in the NMCP's IRS program, and establish a robust insecticide resistance management system.

PMI began support for IRS activities in Zimbabwe in 2012 by conducting a Supplemental Environmental Assessment (SEA), 2012-2016, to the Programmatic Environmental Assessment, to ensure that IRS activities will not adversely impact the environment, people, or bio-diversity in the country. The GoZ and the NMCP were not interested in PMI's initial goal of completing a SEA that would include DDT districts; therefore, PMI support was only limited to districts which do not spray DDT.

In November, 2013, USAID's Global Environmental Management Support Program conducted a field evaluation on environmental compliance of the Africa Indoor Residual Spraying (AIRS) Project in Zimbabwe. The aim of this field environmental evaluation was to enhance implementation of the Zimbabwe AIRS Project in accordance with the Environmental Best Management Practices and to enhance adherence to 22 Code of Federal Regulation 216 or CFR 216 of USAID's environmental policies.

**Table 9: PMI-supported IRS activities 2012 – 2017]**

| Calendar Year | Number of Districts Sprayed | Insecticide Used | Number of Structures Sprayed | Coverage Rate | Population Protected |
|---|---|---|---|---|---|
| 2012 | 13 (3 provinces) | Pyrethroid | 501,613 | 86% | 1,164,586 |
| 2013 | 25 (7 provinces) | Pyrethroid | 622,300 | 91% | 1,431,643 |
| 2014 | 4 (1 province) | organophosphates | 147,949 | 90.3% | 334,746 |
| 2015* | 4 (1 province) | organophosphates | 163,922 | - | 350,000 |
| 2016** | 4 (1 province) | organophosphates | 163,922 | - | 350,000 |
| 2017** | 4 (1 province) | organophosphates | 163,922 | - | 350,000 |

\* Represents targets based on the draft 2015 IRS work plan.
\*\* Represents projected targets based on national strategic plan and/or discussions with the NMCP.

*Progress during the last 12-18 months*

In November-December 2014, PMI conducted its first full IRS campaign in four selected high burden malaria districts in Manicaland province. The key objective was to demonstrate best practices for IRS programming and implementation by: covering at least 85% of eligible structures in four districts, increasing capacity in IRS at the district, provincial and national level, and continuing support with nation-wide entomological monitoring.

A total of 147,949 structures were sprayed, achieving 90.3% coverage and protecting 334,746 people. With PMI support, 332 spray operators and support staff were trained in spray operations, 70 persons were trained in IRS data collection and quality assurance, 29 persons were trained in commodity securing including stock management, 29 others were also trained in information, education and communication (IEC) Training of Trainers to equip them with skills of improving uptake of IRS by communities, plus 317 persons underwent medical check-ups to assess their fitness to enroll as spray operators.

In 2014 PMI continued with the revitalization of the entomology insectaries at NIHR in Harare and its satellite laboratory, De Beers, in Chiredzi. PMI also funded entomological monitoring, carried out in ten sentinel sites in eight malaria endemic provinces. This included three sentinel sites in Manicaland, two of which were IRS areas sprayed with an organophosphate and one site, where no IRS was applied. In addition, PMI supported the NMCP in monitoring insecticide resistance, vector populations and the residual efficacy of insecticides in areas where national program conducts IRS annually. Two of these seven provinces were sprayed with a pyrethroid and five with DDT.

Between August 2014 and February 2015, PMI supported insecticide resistance testing in seven rural provinces. In Manicaland, there were insufficient numbers of *Anopheles* mosquitoes to carry out the insecticide resistance testing. WHO resistance testing was carried out at six sentinel sites outside Manicaland Province with DDT, lambdacyhalothrin, bendiocarb and primiphos-methyl. Susceptibility testing with lambacyhalothrin indicated resistance, in Matabeleland North, Midlands and Mashonaland West provinces, where mortality ranged between 14-21% Bendiocarb resistance was detected in Matabeleland South (16%) and possible DDT resistance (4.4%) in Masvingo Province.

Currently the residual efficacy for organophosphate monitoring in the two Manicaland sites is being carried out. The first three months of evaluation used field collected *An. gambiae* s.l. due to challenges the NIHR had with maintaining sufficient numbers of susceptible *An. arabiensis* in their insectary to provide the number of mosquitoes required for residual insecticide testing. Bioassays conducted 24-48 hr. post-spray showed 100% mortality indicating that there was an adequate quantity of insecticides applied during the IRS.

Testing over the next two months indicated a slight decrease in mortality at the Chakohwa site to 99.5% in December and to 97% in January 2015. The decline in the Burma Valley site was higher with a decrease in residual efficacy to 90% and 88% at two months post-spray. At the Chakohwa site, cement plastered walls showed the greatest decline during the two months post-spray compared brick and painted walls. In Burma Valley, decline in residual activity was highest in painted walls followed by brick and cement plaster walls. As of February 2015, the NIHR was able to produce some susceptible mosquitoes which allows some houses to be tested using both field collected and susceptible colony mosquitoes. Monitoring will continue until two successive months of testing indicate an average of < 80% mosquito mortality in the ten houses monitored.

Longitudinal vector monitoring was conducted using pyrethrum spray collections (PSC) and CDC light traps (LT). At three months post-spray, PSC collections in Burma Valley declined from an average of 1.2 *An. funestus* mosquitoes per room pre-spray to 0.06 *An. funestus* /room. *An. gambiae* s.l. is the main vector found in Chakohwa and at the non-spray site of Mukamba. One mosquito was collected at Chakohwa and none in Mukamba during the same time period. Similarly LT collections in Burma Valley also showed a decrease in indoor collections from an average of 1.7 *An. funestus*/trap pre-IRS to zero mosquitoes. Both the PSC and LT collections indicate a decrease in vector density after IRS, however the increase in LT collections outdoors from an average of 0.33 *An. funestus*/trap pre-IRS to 2.17 *An. funestus*/trap, one month after IRS may indicate an excito-repellency effect of the organophosphate. LT collections also collected no mosquitoes in Chakohwa and Mukamba.

In the other sentinel sites where the NMCP is conducting IRS, both PSC and LT collections showed that vector density was low pre-IRS, except at the Kamhororo sentinel site in Midlands Province. PSC indoor collection was at an average of 2.94 mosquitoes/room and LT outdoor collections at 7.33 mosquitoes/trap (no mosquitoes were collected indoors by LT). A general decrease in mosquito densities was noted two months post-IRS except for Kamhororo where both indoor and outdoor LT collections increased to an average of 9.33 and 3.83 mosquitoes/trap respectively. This increase could be due to a combination of the natural increase in mosquito populations due to the rains and possible vector resistance to DDT used for IRS in this province, as indicated by the WHO resistance testing.

Mosquitoes used in the insecticide resistance testing and collected in the longitudinal vector monitoring are being analyzed using molecular assays for mosquito species identification. In addition, mosquitoes are being tested for malaria parasite infections using immuno-diagnostic assays. The International Centres of Excellence for Malaria Research (ICEMR) is conducting studies in malaria transmission and the impact of control efforts in Southern Africa. Their focus is also in Manicaland where PMI is supporting IRS. During March 2013 to May 2014, ICEMR's entomological monitoring identified the major vector in Mutasa District as *An. funestus* s.s and to a lesser extent *An. leesoni*. The malaria infection rate of the mosquitoes collected was 6.72%.

*Plans and justification*

PMI will continue to concentrate on a robust, full package of IRS implementation in the highest burden province of Manicaland. Unless otherwise requested by the NMCP to refocus PMI support to other districts to achieve greater impact, this shall be the third year PMI will support a full IRS package in the four districts of Manicaland province. The USG restrictions on directly funding the GoZ, along with an approved SEA which only covers non-DDT districts, has restricted PMI's ability to respond to all of the IRS needs for the entire country. The idea is to demonstrate a safe and effective IRS program that other districts in Zimbabwe can learn from. This commitment on the part of PMI is understood to be short-term, to be revisited after two to three years. PMI's contributions to environmental compliance and other cross-cutting efforts, such as entomological monitoring, including insecticide susceptibility monitoring, M&E, and BCC will continue nationwide. However, operational support (training, procurement, etc.) will be limited to only Manicaland. PMI's increased investments in entomological monitoring will provide timely and ample data to inform all malaria partners of the vector situation in Zimbabwe.

*Proposed activities with FY 2016 funding: ($4,940,000)*

PMI will continue funding the IRS full package for four of the seven districts in Manicaland. This will continue demonstrating a model IRS program that other districts can learn from. Districts not supported by PMI will be supported via the Global Fund New Funding Model, with both areas under the leadership of the NMCP. While the non-Manicaland districts will not receive direct PMI support for operations, they will receive indirect support via inclusion in national-level IRS activities, such as: higher-level training, national review and planning meetings, and technical assistance with environmental practices, entomological surveillance, BCC and M&E.

Specific activities to be supported by PMI with FY 2016 funding include:

- *Support spray operations:* Support the full package implementation of a model IRS program in four of the seven districts in Manicaland, spraying approximately 163,922 structures, and protecting approximately 350,000 people. Full package support will include procurement of organophosphate insecticide and equipment, training, operational logistics, environmental compliance, and overall technical assistance to the NCMP. (*$4,500,000*)

- *Entomological surveillance and monitoring:* PMI will continue to support entomological surveillance, including insecticide susceptibility monitoring, in sixteen existing rural sites, plus three urban sites: Mutare, Harare and Bulawayo. PMI plans to expand entomological laboratory capacity beyond MOHCC in order to encourage diversity and alternatives in case the existing capacity at NIHR fails to cope (see HSS section). Entomological surveillance activities will include adult and larval mosquito surveillance; assessing the impact of vector control activities, insecticide resistance monitoring, bioassays to determine IRS longevity on treated surfaces as well as determining the resting and feeding preferences of the vector mosquitoes in and around the sentinel sites. *($400,000)*

- *Procure entomological supplies:* PMI will provide insecticide resistance monitoring equipment and laboratory reagents for entomological activities to the central NIHR and De Beers laboratories. *($11,000)*

- *Technical assistance to PMI IRS activities*: Two CDC technical assistance visits to support entomology, including enhanced insecticide resistance monitoring shall be funded. *($29,000)*

### 3. Malaria in pregnancy

*NMCP/PMI objectives*

Control of malaria in pregnancy (MIP) was adopted as a policy in Zimbabwe in 2004 to be implemented in the moderate to high-burden malaria transmission areas, with 30 districts designated for MIP interventions (see Figure 4 for map of intermittent preventive treatment in pregnancy [IPTp] recommended districts). Additionally, IPTp may be used in specific, localized areas in the medium to low burden districts that are adjacent to high burden districts where there is focal transmission of malaria. For example, senior health officials may note increased malaria cases and request IPTp to protect patients. Also, a woman from a high burden district may seek ANC services in a nearby lower burden area. While SP will be delivered to the facility, its consumption will be monitored. If SP is not consumed, it will not be restocked. The prevention of MIP policy was a three-pronged approach that recommended IPTp with three doses of SP as the drug of choice, distribution and promotion of use of LLINs during pregnancy, and early and effective diagnosis and treatment of clinical malaria. In 2014, the NMCP adopted the latest WHO guidelines for IPTp which recommend administration of IPTp at every ANC visit starting as early as possible in the second trimester and up until the day of delivery, as long as doses are given at least four weeks apart. Adoption of the WHO guidelines will simplify the implementation of IPTp for health workers and likely increase the uptake of IPTp. Each dose of SP is to be administered under a health worker's observation. The policy states that pregnant women on co-trimoxazole prophylaxis should not be administered IPTp. Additionally, with the piloting of continuous LLIN distribution in 2014, ANC clinics are an outlet and pregnant women are to receive a net at their first booking.

According to the national guidelines iron and folate should be routinely given to all pregnant women at ANC starting with their first visit or 12 weeks gestation, whichever is earlier. The doses are elemental iron 60 mg and folic acid 0.4 mg prescribed as one co-formulated tablet daily. In the past there were problems with stockouts but these drugs are now included in the primary care packages.

Antenatal attendance in Zimbabwe is very high with 90% of pregnant women visiting ANC at least once during pregnancy, 65% visiting ANC four or more times, and 65% of pregnant women delivering at a health facility (DHS 2010-11). The 2012 MIS showed that 48% of pregnant women attending ANC in the 30 target IPTp districts received SP and 35% received two or more doses of SP. Sleeping under an LLIN is part of the MIP strategy, and among women of child-bearing age (15-49 years) 49% slept under an LLIN the night preceding the survey according to the 2012 MIS. The NMSP target for the proportion of pregnant women who will receive at least two doses of IPTp and sleep under an LLIN is 85%.

To improve the prevention of MIP and the use of ANC and IPTp, NMCP uses VHWs to educate women at the community level. This strategy supplements facility-based patient education and care services and BCC efforts. Even though VHWs do not give IPTp in the communities, they do advise pregnant women on MIP and encourage early antenatal visits, uptake of IPTp, timely presentation at antenatal care, and consistent use of LLINs. Despite challenges with consistent recording of training attendance, more recent reports from NMCP indicate that 1,325 (20%) of the required 6,600 VHWs had been trained in RDT and ACT treatment use by the end of 2011. Additionally, Global Fund supported VHW training, reaching 90 in 2010 and 2,893 in 2011.

Treatment of uncomplicated malaria in pregnant women is quinine plus clindamycin during the first trimester. If these drugs are unavailable, the recommendation is to use artemether-lumefantrine (AL), which is the first-line ACT. Women in subsequent trimesters are to be treated with AL. With the recent adoption of a second-line ACT, patients in any trimester of pregnancy who do not respond to the first-line treatment should be treated with the second-line treatment which is artesunate-amodiaquine (AS/AQ).

If a woman develops severe malaria during her first trimester, current policy is to treat her with intravenous quinine until she is able to take oral medicines. At that time, she is to be given quinine plus clindamycin to complete a seven day course of treatment for both medicines. If the woman is in her second or third trimester, she is to be given intravenous artesunate initially. Once able to tolerate it, she will switch to oral AL to complete a three-day course with this medicine.

Coordination with maternal/reproductive health programs has been on an *ad hoc* basis since a formal joint meeting was held in 2011. With the change in case management guidelines, efforts are being made to increase this coordination.

**Figure 4: Map of IPTp recommended districts, 2014, Zimbabwe**

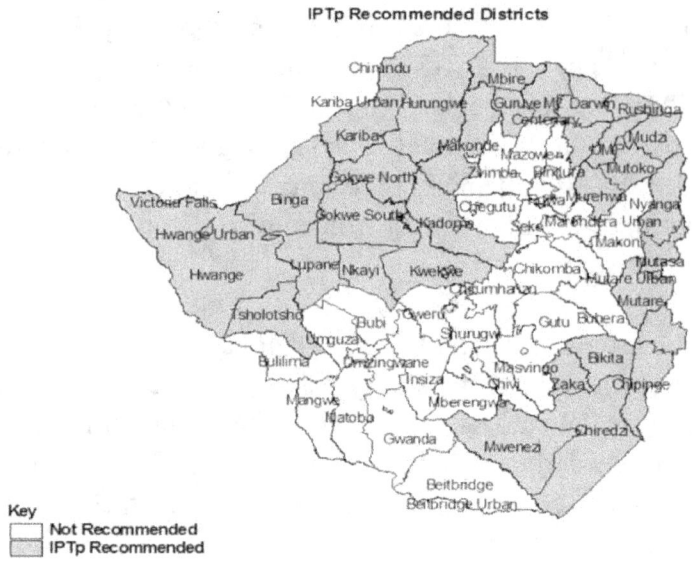

*Progress since PMI was launched*

Annually, PMI has supported the forecasted needs for SP and to date has procured approximately 2.2 million SP treatments. The SP and primary care packages are delivered through the ZIPS, which has helped improve problems with stockouts. Additionally, PMI has supported both facility-based and VHW training and supportive supervision for malaria case management including prevention, intermittent preventive treatment, and treatment of MIP. The VHWs are taught about MIP and broader case management issues, integrating with iCCM, MCCM, and MCH training. During FY 2012-2014, PMI supported the training of 1,683 health workers in IPTp. Global Fund has also continued its support for VHW training and taught 1,142 in 2012 and 215 in 2013. While the total VHWs trained (7,348) exceeds the 6,600 estimated number of VHWs, there has been attrition and recruitment of new VHWs as the VHW program continues to expand. Consequently, there is a known gap in training, with not all VHWs having been trained in community malaria case management.

There has been slight improvement in MIP indicators, with a 2013 case management audit showing 61% and 2014 Health Management Information System (HMIS) data indicating 66% of pregnant women in the IPTp targeted areas took at least two doses of SP. A 2013 PSI Trac Survey reported 68% of pregnant women slept under an ITN the night before the survey. While these improvements are encouraging, they are below the NMSP target of 85%.

*Progress during the last 12-18 months*

PMI continues to support the pharmaceutical and supply chain management (PSM) through ZIPS and ZAPS. The systems distribute SP, iron and folate in the primary care packages, and other commodities for diagnosis and treatment of malaria. While these distribution systems have helped alleviate stockouts, they still remain. One challenge is lack of timely and accurate stock management to allow for redistribution of SP, primarily from facilities that have not used their stock to a higher burdened location. Additionally, delays in deliveries from manufacturers impacted SP distribution. In 2014, approximately 800,000 treatments were procured and distributed and over half a million will be in 2015.

PMI has supported workforce training of both facility-based and village health workers. Manicaland Province conducted a training gap analysis in 2014 and identified the need for 1,400 VHWs to be trained. PMI exceeded that target by training 1,464 VHWs, and 196 nurse aides, 58% of the provincial gap. For the first time, 47 district and provincial level staff from various disciplines were selected and trained to become VHW trainers. Consistent with the partner's objective to support supervision, 20 VHWs were oriented to conduct supportive supervision visits to other VHWs.

PMI partners have supported facility-based health workers and VHWs training on the revised IPTp and malaria case management guidelines. Those VHWs previously trained are being updated on the new policy and others will receive the information for the first time. Facility-based workers have begun receiving training in prevention and management of malaria in pregnancy as part of their malaria case management training (more information in case management section). Malaria case management training materials for both cadres include background information on and revised treatment guidelines for IPTp and MIP. The NMCP is working to have similar job aids disseminated to both general clinics and ANC areas.

PMI has outlined a number of activities that a new partner will conduct starting with FY15 funds that will address a number of issues related to MIP. These include $50,000 to support a rapid assessment to identify key facilitators and barriers to IPTp uptake and ways to strengthen coordination between NMCP and Reproductive Health stakeholders. The results of this work will help with the design of future activities such as the development and delivery of BCC messages to increase demand for and provision of IPTp and other preventive measures.

PMI's activities will also include using $300,000 allocated for M&E activities that will support, among other things, the revision of data collection tools and reporting on the number of IPTp doses taken by women. The revision of tools will be discussed with stakeholders working in other disease sectors to strive for an integrated efficient approach and product.

## Commodity gap analysis

**Table 10. SP Gap Analysis for Malaria in Pregnancy**

| Calendar Year | 2015 | 2016 | 2017 |
|---|---|---|---|
| Total Population | 13, 497,019 | 13, 645,486 | 13,795,586 |
| Estimated population in malaria endemic areas | 6,786,344 | 6,842,796 | 6,918,067 |
| **SP Needs** | | | |
| Total number of pregnant women attending ANC | 223,047 | 225,500 | 227,980 |
| **Total SP Need (in treatments)** | **892,188** | **902,000** | **911,920** |
| **Partner Contributions** | | | |
| SP carried over (deficit) from previous year | 510,407 | 449,902 | 136,371 |
| SP from MOH | 0 | 0 | 0 |
| SP from Global Fund | 47,533 | 48,900 | 128,966 |
| SP from Other Donors | 0 | 0 | 0 |
| SP planned with PMI funding | 784,150 | 539,515 | 161,519 |
| **Total SP Available** | 1,342,090 | 1,038,317 | 426,802 |
| **Total SP Surplus (Gap)** | 449,902 | 136,371 | (485,118) |

Footnotes: Pregnant women are assumed to be approximately 4% total population. For quantification, the assumption is that 50% pregnancies will occur in malarious areas and consumption data are used. It is assumed that all pregnant women attending ANC will receive four treatments.

## Plans and justification

With FY 2016 funds, PMI will continue to procure and distribute SP, planning on approximately 161,000 treatments. The projected need and PMI contribution may be refined after reviewing progress toward increased uptake by women and updated consumption data. PMI will also provide support to the MIP implementing districts for the training and supportive supervision of district, health facility, and community level staff on the revised IPTp and MIP implementation guidelines. This training is part of comprehensive maternal health care delivery training which aims to improve the uptake of IPTp by improving demand for ANC services. Other MIP topics covered by the training will include LLIN promotion and treatment of malaria for pregnant women. The number of VHWs in Manicaland increased to 2,134 by April 2015 and is expected to rise further. PMI will continue to document progress toward targeted numbers of workers trained, aiming to provide refresher training to the approximately 1,400 VHWs already trained and reach approximately 700 who have never been trained in MCCM. The NMCP will also use Global Fund resources to train facility-based workers and possibly VHWs. Case management audits, PSM consumption and health facility utilization data, supervisory visit reports, plus data from the 2016 MIS will be used to monitor success. PMI will also provide technical assistance to the NMCP to improve the forecasting and distribution of SP to the target health facilities to ensure a stable supply.

PMI will engage with NMCP regarding opportunities to update facility records, registers, and HMIS to capture the total number of doses of SP given to women.

As part of PMI's support for malaria BCC activities, PMI will support the use of data from the assessment of barriers and facilitators to IPTp uptake and other evidence to guide the development of BCC plans for prevention of MIP and knowledge of and adherence to updated treatment guidelines for cases of malaria in pregnant women.

*Proposed activities with FY 2016 funding: ($33,919)*

- *Procurement of SP*: PMI will procure approximately 161,000 treatments of SP for distribution to health facilities located in the target districts for IPTp. Technical assistance will also be provided to improve the quantification and forecasting of SP to ensure a stable supply annually. *($33,919)*

- *Support health worker training and supervision in MIP*: PMI will support the training of health workers in the revised IPTp and implementation guidelines. Support will cover the districts designated for MIP interventions to guide pregnant women to follow the current WHO recommended IPTp SP dosing, use of LLINs during pregnancy, and early and effective diagnosis and treatment of malaria. The training will also include data recording and reporting. This training and supportive supervision support will benefit health center nurses and ANC nurses in the district hospitals. As part of the integrated iCCM/MCH/MCCM activities, nurse aides and VHWs will increase their knowledge of new practice guidelines as well. Although a final target has not been set, it is anticipated that approximately 600 VHWs will be targeted to receive initial training and 1,400 VHWs will receive updated training to meet approximately 100% of the expected growth in this cadre in the province representing about a third of VHWs nationwide. *(Costs included in case management: diagnosis and treatment)*

- *Support for MIP BCC activities*: PMI will support activities focusing on community sensitization, improved IPTp uptake, and other preventive measures such as the use of LLINs during pregnancy. *(Costs included in behavior change communication)*

4. **Case management**

   a. **Diagnosis and Treatment**

*NMCP/PMI objectives*

Since August 2010, the NMCP's policy has been to have parasitological confirmation of all suspected malaria cases by microscopy or RDT before prescribing treatment. Exceptions to this policy are made in the case of malaria epidemics or stockouts of diagnostic tests at the health facility. Rapid diagnostic tests and/or microscopy are typically used for malaria diagnosis at all health facilities, with the exception of primary health facilities where only RDTs are available. Monospecies *P.f.* RDTs have been used in 80% of the country with multispecies ones used in the pre-elimination region of Matebeleland South Province. Multispecies RDTs will be procured by Global Fund, and possibly GoZ, for use in pre-elimination areas.

Zimbabwe has seen an increase in reported cases in 2013 and 2014 compared to 2011 but in the first months of 2015, cases have decreased compared to the same periods in 2014. It is anticipated that with the continued deployment of malaria interventions, including the use of OPs in some of the highest burdened districts, that reported cases will decrease by 10% each year.

Given the policy of parasitological confirmation and the predominant use of RDTs, the NMCP assumes that there are three suspected cases of malaria for each confirmed case. Additionally, in pre-elimination districts, which will increase from 7 in 2014 to 20 by 2017, the assumption is for every seven suspected cases tested, one will be positive and RDTs will also be used in case investigations.

Commodities for diagnosis and treatment are pooled in the national PSM system, regardless of funding source and distributed primarily to high burden areas with specific items going to pre-elimination areas as stated above. Also, since patients are mobile and can present or be referred to facilities in non-endemic areas, some commodities are distributed to those areas as well so health workers may have resources to appropriately diagnose and manage malaria patients.

Zimbabwe has 5 central hospitals, 8 provincial hospitals and 68 district hospitals, 4 of which are situated in urban areas; all of these facilities have laboratories. The Department for Laboratory Service is located under the Division of Curative Services of the MOHCC, and is funded primarily by the GoZ. This department is responsible for policy formulation and organizes supervision and refresher training of laboratory personnel. It also recommends quantities of microscopy and laboratory supplies. The department's activities are conducted in collaboration with the Tuberculosis Reference Laboratory in Bulawayo, National Virology Laboratory at the University of Zimbabwe Medical School, and the National Microbiology Reference Laboratory (NMRL). Through Global Fund support, about 200 microscopes were purchased under the TB program. The Ministry supplies laboratory reagents but the quantities are usually not sufficient to meet all needs.

Zimbabwe has three main cadres of facility-based laboratory staff: clinical scientists with a masters or doctorate-level degree; general laboratory scientists with a bachelor's degree from the university; and state certified laboratory technicians who receive two years of training post-high school at the polytechnic level. A professional registry, the Medical Laboratory and Clinical Scientist Council, accredits personnel before they can practice. There is a critical need for more laboratory scientists and technicians. The microscopists currently employed in the health services are paid through the Global Fund Round 8 so at the end of the grant in December 2014 it will be difficult to retain them without future donor or government funding. While the government hiring freeze has ended and staff who leave may be replaced, recruitment takes time and there remains a freeze on the creation of new positions.

According to the NMCP, parasitological diagnosis of malaria has been fully rolled out to all health facilities and technical assistance visits in 2013 to a sample of facilities confirmed the availability of malaria microscopy and RDTs. All of the 12 facilities visited consistently had available microscopy, RDTs, or both. As a result, and as required by policy, all malaria cases should be laboratory confirmed. Health centers have mainly RDTs, but a few of the health centers visited also had microscopy capability with trained microscopists who perform both TB and malaria microscopy. In facilities with both RDTs and microscopy, RDTs are mainly used at the outpatient department for testing suspected malaria cases prior to them seeing the clinician.

No in-country entity currently provides malaria RDT QA/QC. Through support from another donor, an internationally-based organization is providing laboratory services including laboratory monitoring for those with HIV/AIDS as well as HIV Rapid Test Kit QA and technical assistance for the national laboratory services and the partner which previously provided malaria diagnostic QA/QC. The organization will enhance this assistance with the assignment of a consultant in country for three years having started mid-2014. As capacity increases, PMI, NMCP, and NMRL will be able to critically assess the capacity of in-country entities and work to build a more robust and structured malaria diagnostic QA/QC program.

An additional missing piece of QA/QC is lot testing of RDTs, which currently is not being done. However, determination of a national laboratory's capacity to do so is being explored.

Malaria diagnostic capacity using RDTs has been strengthened since the 2009 national policy allowing VHWs to use ACTs and RDTs and the inclusion of RDT training in case management training provided to health workers and VHWs. However, initial limited funding support of village and facility-based worker training and procurement of laboratory diagnostic commodities, including RDTs, impeded progress in case management. More recently, near- to adequate supplies of RDTs have been procured with donor support. With the recent Global Fund award, there should continue to be adequate supplies (Table 11).

Training, supervision, and procurement efforts have contributed to increased parasitological confirmation of cases. Historically, malaria case reporting data has included both laboratory-confirmed and unconfirmed cases. Since 2005, the number of cases diagnosed clinically is decreasing whereas parasitological diagnosis is increasing. In 2005, only 8.5% of clinical cases were tested while in 2013 the percentage had increased to 97.9%.

In 2004, Zimbabwe adopted AL as its first-line treatment for uncomplicated malaria. In 2014, the country revised its treatment guidelines to align with WHO recommendations. Consequently, it adopted AS/AQ as its second-line ACT for uncomplicated malaria, and adopted IV artesunate as the first-line option for severe malaria. These cases are assumed to be 5% of the cases reported upon presentation as well as 5% of uncomplicated cases that will progress to severe. Some stocks of quinine will be maintained to combine with a second drug as an alternative for first trimester pregnant women and in the case of stockouts of artesunate. Artesunate suppository use for pre-referral treatment of severe malaria, especially in children and at the community level, was also adopted.

It is anticipated that AS/AQ will be provided to referral facilities first in areas where the health workers have received training on the revised treatment guidelines. The quantities will be small to start because the MOHCC has quinine stocks it will use before they expire. Rural health centers will receive AS/AQ stocks but they will not be issued to village health workers. PMI expects to complement support from other donors, mainly Global Fund and meet the need for the first line ACT allowing for support for the introduction of the second line ACT.

To decrease transmission, the country will also introduce the use of low-dose primaquine for its gametocytocidal effect in infections in low transmission/elimination areas, initially with robust pharmacovigilance. It is assumed that 15% of cases will need this medicine. The Global Fund has supported procurement of 53,000 tablets of primaquine, 15mg base, in 2015 and 46,000 tablets in 2016. These new policies have been incorporated into training manuals, training curricula and supervision checklists, and revised treatment guidelines. Procurement of the adopted medicines began in late 2014.

In 2009-10, the NMCP adopted a policy of community case management for malaria and conducted a pilot study to evaluate this program. Trained VHWs follow an algorithm to test all suspected cases with an RDT and treat those with positive results with an ACT. Based on this pilot, the NMCP has been scaling up the training of community VHWs to implement community-based treatment on a national scale in malaria endemic districts. The VHWs are selected from their ward by the community. They receive training in iCCM, which has a malaria component, as well as focused training in community malaria case management to deliver care in an integrated manner. The primary health facility staff is responsible for supervising the VHWs and their data collection. The NMCP planned to train 6,600 VHWs in malaria case management by 2013. As the VHW network expands, it is assumed that they will be very accessible to community members, and at times more accessible than a health facility. Consequently, diagnosis and treatment rendered by VHWs can help decrease the patient load at health facilities and increase timely diagnosis and management. The resources that would have otherwise been used at the facility level will be used at the community level.

Despite the institution of community-based malaria case management, overall expansion of case management capacity has been hampered by the difficult national economic conditions that have resulted in high turnover of health workers leaving inadequate numbers of qualified and trained workers. A review of historical records shows that of 18,000 health workers who were earmarked for malaria training (case management/MIP/RDTs), approximately half have ever been trained. While it is encouraging that the GoZ removed the hiring freeze at least twice in the past three years on some nursing positions and 2,000 were hired, this group of workers will also need to be trained. At a minimum, the NMCP had a target of training 500 health workers in the calendar years 2014 and 2015 which should help meet the need to cover untrained health workers in the 47 high burden districts.

The NMCP has been developing its subnational pre-elimination activities with support from partners other than PMI starting with an assessment of M&E capacity in Matebeleland South in 2013. This was followed by a strategic planning workshop where provincial strategies to reach elimination were outlined. A framework was drafted by the NMCP and partners. Additional activities have included the development of a mobile reporting system. This digital surveillance system was designed to improve data quality, data timeliness and completeness in reporting, and data use. Personnel were trained to use the system that was rolled out in September 2014 in the seven pre-elimination districts.

Future plans include the expansion of pre-elimination activities to a total of 20 districts with the support of Global Fund and other partners. The NMCP is conducting a capacity assessment of the new districts using a multiple indicator tool to assess areas such as case management, M&E, surveillance, and the community case worker system to help develop expansion plans. Also, the digital surveillance system will be upgraded to ensure it is on an open source platform owned by NMCP and developers and data will integrate into the DHIS2.

To build upon advances to date and prepare for the future, the NMCP is planning to create a malaria reference center which, once established, will provide timely data for pre-elimination efforts, supervise national surveillance systems, and provide laboratory analysis services for the entire Southern African region. In addition to improved laboratory infrastructure, this endeavor will require enhanced human resource capacity, focused on laboratory analysis skills.

PMI will continue to focus its support on reducing malaria in the highest burdened areas while other partners support efforts to decrease transmission and eliminate the disease in lower transmission and pre-elimination areas. However, PMI participates in discussions and provides technical input into pre-elimination efforts in country and the region, e.g., through the Elimination 8 Initiative and stays abreast of topics, needs, and plans. By doing so, PMI will be in the position to annually evaluate its role in providing technical and other support, if indicated, toward the pre-elimination strategy in Zimbabwe.

*Progress since PMI was launched*

PMI has supported the procurement of malaria commodities including RDTs and malaria medicines. To date PMI has procured 6.6 million RDTs, 3.7 million ACT treatments, 120,000 quinine treatments, 32,400 rectal suppositories and 183,000 vials of injectable artesunate. To enhance health worker performance, PMI has supported facility-based health worker training and supportive supervision. PMI is also supporting the training and supervision of VHWs in MCCM. This training is integrated with iCCM and MCH activities and platforms. The strategies include MCCM training, supportive supervision, including by peers, documentation and reporting, quality improvement, and integrating MCCM and MCH. Additionally, the problem of a lack of a standardized malaria curriculum was corrected when a PMI implementing partner facilitated its creation.

Recent NMCP reports indicate that more than 8,000 (more than 44%) of the estimated 18,000 health workers were trained in malaria case management and M&E and 1,325 (20%) of the required 6,600 VHWs were trained in RDTs and ACT treatment use by the end of 2011. Global Fund supported the training of a total of 4,325 VHWs between 2010 and 2013. During 2013, the NMCP trained a total of 1,412 health workers in case management, RDT use, and malaria in pregnancy, exceeding their target of 1,112. PMI supported the training of an additional 300 heath workers. This total of 1,712 workers is 9.5% of the 18,000 health workers.

PMI has supported BCC activities to increase lay person knowledge of malaria and to encourage early treatment seeking.

*Progress during the last 12-18 months*

PMI conducted a training gap analysis in early 2014 in Manicaland to assess gaps in malaria case (facility and community) case management. Training registers and health information databases were cited by participating district health staff as sources of information. In the seven districts in the province, there were 4,976 workers in the categories of doctors, nurses, nurse aides, EHTs, VHWs, and SHMs. Of that number, 3,055 (65%) lacked training. The gaps ranged from 32% (449/1,410) among nurses and EHTs (37/117), 68% (1,405/1,968) among VHWs, 85% (34/40) among doctors to 100% of the 993 SHMs.

PMI partners met or exceeded their targets for training nurse aides, VHWs, and SHMs. One hundred ninety-six nurse aides were also trained, exceeding the target of 150. By training 1,464 VHWs, the gap in Manicaland has been reduced from 68% to 31% of the increased denominator of 2,136 in April 2015. Also, the gap for SHMs was reduced from 100% to 56% with the training of 436 in this cadre. The SHMs will form school health clubs to educate students about malaria prevention and treatment. Other stakeholders have also contributed to malaria prevention and case management training by training VHWs, SHMs, supporting NMCP's supervision of community based health workers by EHTs.

Various partners have documented improvements in pre- and post-training knowledge of malaria prevention and case management. For example, in 2014 115 VHWs scored an average of 60% on the pre-test and 69% on the post-test. Of the 254 VHWs trained in 2013-2014 the partner noted

46

that only 27% of the cohort scored above 50% on the pre-test but the proportion increased to 90% on the post-test.

To expand training capacity, PMI initiated training of trainers for VHWs and developed and printed 3,000 participant and 300 facilitator manuals for VHW training. These materials will be used in Manicaland to train VHWs new to MCCM and update the 1,464 VHWs trained on the old guidelines. In an effort to standardize training, the majority of the facilitator and some participant manuals will be sent to the NMCP for distribution to provinces and UMCOR and the United Methodist Church, who also train some VHWs. The NMCP will use Global Fund resources for training and supervision.

Training on the new treatment guidelines began with the drafting of participant and facilitators manuals for facility-based workers. Ten thousand were sent to health facilities nationwide. In the first half of 2015, 159 trainers from multiple disciplines, primarily from admitting hospitals and the uniformed forces, were trained, leaving a national gap of 34% (81/240). The goal was to have at least three sets of trainers per province. While these trainers will primarily train other facility-based staff, the trainers may also be used to train VHWs.

Additionally, a 1-day curriculum was designed and over 4,700 of 6,000 (78%) staff, mostly nurses from admitting hospitals, were trained. These workers are expected to cascade training to other team members. The goal for this training is to reach 6,000 workers who are assumed to represent half of the 12,000 admitting hospital-based workers, out of 18,000 health workers nationwide. A two-and-a-half day course was developed for workers at other levels in the health care system. Out of a target of 6,000 workers in rural health facilities, PMI trained 700 and NMCP trained 1,080, with Global Fund support.

After significant delays, the therapeutic efficacy monitoring teams began collecting samples for evaluation at six sites in mid-2013. PMI supported four sites and WHO two sites. Unfortunately 2013 did not yield sufficient numbers of cases for the study. Between February and May 2014, data were collected from four PMI-supported sites (Dindi, Hauna, Nyamhunga, and Simatelele) with two additional sites supported by WHO. Preliminary PCR-corrected data indicated 97.5% (391 out 401 persons from six sites) of participants had adequate clinical and parasitological response. Final PCR-corrected results are pending.

The MOHCC considers cross border malaria a priority area for investigation so evidence-based decisions can be made to decrease the malaria burden, which is highest in three provinces bordering Mozambique. Discussions with Mozambican NMCP counterparts are underway and joint meetings planned. NMCP and other partners recognize that certain populations may not be reached by or able to access the prevention and treatment interventions that are used. These groups include miners, gold panners, seasonal workers, cross border traders, rotating teachers, and residents who transit to and settle in new unofficially recognized areas or in new areas opened up after land reform decisions. Also, some people move between a permanent home and a temporary one when conducting economic activities and may miss out on benefits from malaria interventions.. These groups are known to be in border areas in the highest burdened provinces. Currently, a PMI partner is embarking on a situational analysis to better characterize the magnitude and characteristics of these groups; the interventions available to and accessed by them; and their attitudes, knowledge and practices regarding malaria prevention and care seeking. Residents from Zimbabwe and Mozambique will be interviewed. It is anticipated that the results obtained will provided needed information to help NMCP and partners, including those in Mozambique, design evidence-based activities to address these issues. PMI will also work with the Elimination 8 group which was recently awarded a Global Fund grant and is soliciting proposals to supplement the work of individual countries to coordinate activities.

*Commodity gap analysis*

## Table 11: RDT Gap Analysis

| Calendar Year | 2015 | 2016 | 2017 |
|---|---|---|---|
| **RDT Needs** | | | |
| Target population at risk for malaria | 6,786,344 | 6,842,796 | 6,918,067 |
| Total number projected malaria cases* | 481,991 | 433,791 | 390,412 |
| Percent of fever cases confirmed with microscopy | 5 | 5 | 5 |
| Percent of fever cases confirmed with RDT | 98 | 98 | 98 |
| **Total RDT Needs** | **3,575,628** | **3,177,565** | **2,859,809** |
| **Partner Contributions** | | | |
| RDTs carried over (deficit) from previous year | 2,690,679 | 2,402,551 | 982,550 |
| RDTs from MOH | 0 | 0 | 0 |
| RDTs from Global Fund (20% Pan) | 949,500 | 256,600 | 256,600 |
| RDTs from Other Donors | 0 | 0 | 0 |
| RDTs planned with PMI funding | 2,338,000 | 1,500,964 | 1,866,792 |
| **Total RDTs Available** | 5,978,179 | 4,160,115 | 3,105,942 |
| **Total RDT Surplus (Gap)** | 2,402,551 | 982,550 | 246,133 |

Footnotes: The population at risk is counted as those in malaria endemic areas. *The number of fever cases is not measured by NMCP so projected malaria cases are listed. Quantification is based on consumption data. The case burden is assumed to decrease by 10% each year based on use of effective interventions. Cases confirmed by RDT and microscopy are not mutually exclusive.

**Table 12: ACT Gap Analysis**

| Calendar Year | 2015 | 2016 | 2017 |
|---|---|---|---|
| **ACT Needs** | | | |
| Target population at risk for malaria | 6,786,344 | 6,842,796 | 6,918,067 |
| Total projected number of malaria cases | 481,991 | 433,791 | 390,412 |
| **Total ACT Needs** | **1,423,174** | **1,033,145** | **929,209** |
| **Partner Contributions** | | | |
| ACTs carried over (deficit) from previous year | 958,422 | 782,617 | 879,388 |
| ACTs from MOH | 0 | 0 | 0 |
| ACTs from Global Fund | 418,689 | 612,000 | 361,305 |
| ACTs from Other Donors | 0 | 0 | 0 |
| ACTs planned with PMI funding | 826,680 | 517,916 | 517,916 |
| **Total ACTs Available** | **2,205,791** | **1,912,533** | **1,758,609** |
| **Total ACT Surplus (Gap)** | 782,617 | 879,388 | 829,400 |

Footnote: The population at risk is counted as those in malaria endemic areas. Case burden is expected to decrease 10% annually due to effective interventions. Assumed from the projected 2015 case figures that 95% will be uncomplicated. Five percent of those will go to a second line ACT. Assumed breakdown /weight band is 24% infant, 22% toddler, 20% child and 34% adult. Assume 5% severe cases at presentation and 5% of the uncomplicated ones will progress to severe per NMCP data. Quantities for ACTs are based on consumption data. Since no consumption data are available for new drugs to be used for severe malaria, forecasting based on morbidity data - source *The Malaria Medicine and Rapid Diagnostic Test Annual Quantification Report, February 2015, Ministry of Health and Child Care*, page 13.

## *Plans and justification*

PMI will continue supporting case management through procurement of malaria medicines and diagnostic commodities, training and supervision of facility-based and village health workers, and BCC for community members, especially in light of revised treatment guidelines and availability of new medicines. It is anticipated that AS/AQ will be provided to referral facilities first in areas where the health workers have received training on the revised treatment guidelines. The quantities will be small to start because the MOHCC has quinine stocks it will use before they expire. Rural health centers will receive AS/AQ stocks but they will not be issued to village health workers. PMI expects to complement support from other donors, mainly Global Fund and meet the need for the first line ACT allowing for support for the introduction of the second line ACT.

As described above, the NMCP recognizes that certain populations may not be reached by or able to access malaria treatment interventions. The MOHCC is investigating cross border malaria so evidence-based decisions can be made to decrease the malaria burden.

Active case detection and enhanced surveillance in pre-elimination areas, including newly identified districts, will be supported. The VHW network will be assessed to determine its ability to support malaria control and pre-elimination efforts. The results of recent work on cross border malaria and the identification of any gaps in malaria protection and treatment will help guide activities to meet service gaps for mobile populations. Additionally, PMI will support university capacity to conduct epidemiological and entomological analyses and at the same time build work force capacity among students and staff.

*Proposed activities with FY 2016 funding: ($3,472,758)*

- *Procure RDTs for malaria diagnosis:* Procure approximately 1.87 million RDTs at $0.53 per test for use at health facilities and by VHWs. *($1,000,000)*
- *Procure ACTs:* Procure approximately 500,000 courses of treatment of AL and 20,000 courses of treatment of ASAQ at an average cost of $1.21 per course. *($594,000)*
- *Procure injectable artesunate for severe malaria drugs:* Procure approximately 166,000 vials of artesunate injectable at $2.60 per vial for use at hospital and health facilities to which patients present or have been referred. Assume 5% presenting cases (60% pediatric, 40% adult) plus 5% uncomplicated becoming severe. *($431,930)*
- *Procure artesunate suppositories:* Procure approximately 59,000 artesunate suppositories, 50% are 200 mg and 50% are 50 mg at an average cost of $0.60 per suppository. The target is to distribute to 3600 VHWs to use before referring the patient. *($36,828)*
- *Procure malaria diagnostic supplies:* Procure laboratory supplies to support malaria diagnostics *($50,000)*
- *Technical assistance visit:* A technical assistance visit will be conducted by a CDC laboratory expert to provide technical support to the NMCP on ongoing diagnostic activities in country. *($10,000)*
- *Facilitate supportive supervision for health facility workers:* Support NMCP to conduct supportive supervision on malaria case management for primary health facility staff and limited refresher training; support real time active case detection and follow up in selected pre-elimination districts. *($500,000)*
- *Assess, train, and supervise VHWs in MCCM:* Assess status and needs of VHW network and ability to support malaria control and pre-elimination activities to inform new project the following year. Support training and supervision on MCCM for VHWs. *($500,000)*
- *Meet service gaps for mobile populations:* PMI will address previously identified gaps in protection and treatment for mobile populations. *($200,000)*
- *Build malaria laboratory capacity:* Continue support to build university laboratory capacity for both epidemiologic and entomologic surveillance sample analysis. This activity will increase access to quality analysis for malaria surveillance activities in

Zimbabwe, while also building human capacity and improving local platforms for teaching critical laboratory skills. *($150,000)*

## b. Pharmaceutical Management

*NMCP/PMI objectives*

Over the past 10 years, MOHCC has developed and implemented a number of supply chains in order to ensure availability of health commodities at facility level. The Directorate of Pharmacy Services (DPS) developed a strategic plan for 2012–2015. The availability of medicines is one of the key performance indicators for the MOHCC. An annual quantification process, including updates every trimester, is led by the DPS in consultation with the NMCP.

To plan for the future, when MOHCC will be responsible for supporting public health supply chain management systems, DPS and Zimbabwe National Family Planning Council have begun looking at the possibility of harmonizing the management of health commodities. The vision is to bring the management of all health commodities under a single unified commodities system for all primary care facilities and also have TB, malaria, and preventive commodities distributed via one system to all levels. The MOHCC's goal is to reduce the number of systems to one or two, and to implement more effective and efficient supply chain operations that are sustainable in the medium to long term. The MOHCC plans to bring about these changes while still ensuring that the needed data is collected, that re-supply takes place according to a defined schedule, and that coverage/order rates and stockout rates remain at or are better than those achieved under the current multiple systems.

The ZIPS, a rolling warehouse concept that uses informed push mechanism, distributes malaria (ACTs, SP, and severe malaria pharmaceuticals), TB, and 26 selected essential medicines and medical supplies (including RDTs) to approximately 1,500 service delivery points quarterly. The ZIPS was piloted in 2009 and quickly rolled out. It allowed for the first time collection of data on consumption, stock on hand, losses and adjustments for malaria commodities. The MOHCC DPS in conjunction with NatPharm provides leadership to the ZIPS, including leading the annual national quantification process and mid-year updates. The quantification of malaria commodities is integrated with that for other program commodities such as TB, HIV/AIDS, drugs for opportunistic infections, and other essential medicines and medical supplies. The MOHCC programs (AIDS, TB, malaria) and partners (Clinton Health Access Initiative [CHAI], UNDP, UNICEF, Elizabeth Glazer Pediatric AIDS Foundation, Supply Chain Management System, and USAID/DELIVER PROJECT) participate and provide input to the quantification.

*Progress since PMI was launched*

PMI has supported procurement and distribution of commodities as well as operational and logistical support for PSM. Activities covered under the ZIPS operations budget line include fuel, maintenance and repairs for delivery trucks and monitoring vehicles, ZIPS forms printing, internet technology hardware and software maintenance, ZIPS mop up training, support and supervision of the distribution system, direct and indirect costs of technical assistance including, but not limited to, maintaining critical positions and field office operations.

Two critical positions include a PSM specialist and the secondment of a pharmacist to DPS. Their technical expertise has helped with coordination of malaria supply chain activities, annual quantification and updates leading to any needed revision in procurements, and support for end-use verification (EUV) surveys, for which the pharmacists is the lead data analyst and reporter. Prior to the initiation of the EUV surveys, PMI supported a stakeholders meeting to explain the process and anticipated outcomes, which enhanced stakeholder buy in and adherence to the quarterly survey schedule. Additionally, PMI supports the Logistics Management Information System (LMIS) and has supported the printing of forms.

To achieve the goal of moving to a unified system, in late 2013, the MOHCC with support from the USAID/DELIVER PROJECT designed an integrated single "assisted ordering pull" system. The ZAPS manages the several categories of products that were previously managed by multiple logistics systems at the primary care level, as well as at secondary and upper levels for selected preventive products. The ZAPS was piloted in Manicaland Province for one year starting April 1, 2014. If the ZAPS pilot project proves successful in generating the same or better level of supply chain performance at lower cost when compared to the existing systems, then ZAPS will replace ZIPS and will be rolled out nationwide.

*Progress during the last 12-18 months*

PMI supported approximately a third of the costs of ZIPS operations and supported the LMIS to complement other donor support. An evaluation of existing distribution systems was conducted by USAID/DELIVER PROJECT as part of a baseline measurement for the evaluation of the ZAPS system. The evaluation collected data for 2013 and the first quarter of 2014 and looked at indicators for performance and costs. With respect to information availability and quality, almost 100% of ZIPS facilities received a quarterly visit. The level of on time and acceptably late (within 90 and 90-120 days after last visit, respectively) data collection and on time delivery was generally good. Levels ranged from 67%-94% with the exception of 2013 Q2 when the level dropped to 30% and 2013 Q4 when the run was skipped. These data show the impact that cash flow challenges at NatPharm present to obtaining essential medicines kits. Commodity availability and inventory management went well in the first half of 2013 with approximately 93% stock of full supply products available on the day of the visit. The levels fell to 83% in Q3 and to 73% in 2014 Q1. The latest results likely reflect the skipped delivery the previous quarter. When stockouts occurred, they generally lasted more than eight days. Overstocking was found to be a concern having been noted in 18%-51% of facilities during the quarters measured. However, the expiry rate for ZIPS products were less than one percent for the entire period measured. All of the existing systems were found to be relatively cost effective. The ZIPS was found to be a mature and mostly well performing system.

Discordance between malaria case (HMIS) and LMIS data presents challenges for the quantification process and the commodity management system. A recent study found that the reasons for the discrepancy between HMIS data and ZIPS data included splitting and combining of ACT by service delivery points, challenges with record keeping including use of different source records and inconsistent record keeping especially during malaria outbreaks, lack of standardized RDT registers, late submission of VHW reports, and poor understanding of malaria case definitions among health workers. PMI will support activities to improve LMIS data quality and commodity management through workshops for district pharmacy managers to improve issues of stock management and record keeping at the facility level. For example, stock counts may be incorrect when all stocks stored in more than one place are not counted, or expired stock is not separated from usable stock, or stockout days are not recorded correctly, affecting average monthly consumption calculations. Also, areas for improvement in team leader performance and data keeping were identified. After reviewing central and district level issues and possible solutions proposed during the workshops, a checklist will be developed to assist the managers in identifying issues at facilities and monitoring their progress in addressing them.

The NMCP's recent adoption of WHO treatment recommendations will result in changes to the supply chain. Increasing the number of products may involve more deliveries to the same number of facilities. The challenge lies in ensuring a good balance between making sure new regimens are available in full supply while minimizing overstocking and possible losses of the old and new products. PMI will support this transition on a phase in, phase out basis. Balancing stock availability is also complicated by the occurrence of outbreaks and unstable epidemic patterns influenced by climate and weather patterns.

Quality lapses in RDTs necessitated procurement changes and training updates on new products. Also, shortages of artesunate and limited supplier capacity of artesunate suppositories on the international market are potential bottlenecks to product delivery. PMI will work with NMCP and partners to analyze the gaps in the supply chain and ensure that both PMI- and Global Fund-supported procurements complement each other. Additionally, as more data become available and are analyzed, more will become known about the success of ZAPS and its potential for expansion nationwide.

### *Plans and justification*

PMI will continue to ensure that malaria commodities, such as ACTs, RDTs, severe malaria medicines, and SP, are available in health facilities through ZIPS and ZAPS. Support will also be given to strengthen and expand supervision and quality assurance. PMI also plans to support the nationwide rollout of ZAPS if it proves to be successful at replacing ZIPS. PMI support will complement that of other donors including pharmaceutical supply chain management training and procurement of SP, ACTs, primaquine, quinine, and RDTs by the Global Fund.

*Proposed activities with FY 2016 funding: ($900,000)*

- *Support approximately 33% of the ZIPS or ZAPS*: Support ZIPS/ZAPS operations to provide ACTs, RDTs, severe malaria medicines, and SP to approximately 1,500 health facilities nationwide. Funds will complement other pharmaceutical and commodities management funding from other partners. PMI support will include operational costs, technical assistance, trainings, quantification support and logistics. *($900,000)*

## 5. Health system strengthening and capacity building

PMI supports a broad array of health system strengthening activities which cut across intervention areas, such as training of health workers, supply chain management and health information systems strengthening, drug quality monitoring, and NCMP capacity building.

*NMCP/PMI objectives*

The NMCP leads Zimbabwe's malaria control efforts through the formulation of policy strategies and the coordination of all partners involved in malaria control in Zimbabwe. The NMCP coordinates malaria activities at all levels, and implements directly at the national and provincial levels. In 2015, the MOHCC became the Principal Recipient for malaria and tuberculosis related activities funded by the Global Fund in Zimbabwe. The NMCP will direct all activities under the malaria grant, reporting to and advising the program coordination unit within the MOHCC. The NMCP collaborates with several partners including USAID, UNICEF, WHO, CDC, CHAI, and other international and local institutions.

The NMCP has demonstrated strong management and planning. Technical areas that NMCP leadership would like to see strengthened within the institution include entomology, vector control, epidemic detection and response, and prevalence estimate mapping or stratification.

Through the Field Epidemiology Training Program (FETP), the University of Zimbabwe trains public health personnel in field epidemiology, data analysis, epidemiologic methods, and use of strategic information to make appropriate health decisions. This is a two-year course, which typically benefits central- and provincial-level MOHCC personnel. At the end of the program, graduates earn a Master of Public Health degree. The University also organizes a short course on leadership and health management for middle-level MOHCC personnel who work at the district level.

*Progress since PMI was launched*

PMI supported a cohort of FETP students that began coursework and training in January 2013 and partnered with the University of Zimbabwe to strengthen the malaria curriculum within the existing FETP program. The goal is to have the supported students receive a malaria-focused education and enhance the malaria competency of the entire class. To date, two students from each cohort have been selected annually. One FETP candidate is assigned to the NMCP under the supervision of the NMCP Director to support their programmatic and monitoring work, and another candidate is assigned to a province under the supervision of the Medical Director to support malaria work at the provincial level. In 2013 and 2014 the FETP conducted eight malaria outbreak investigations in Zimbabwe. These investigations were presented to the NMCP and MOHCC staff during monthly seminars.

In the past four years, PMI has worked with the NIHR, which is a national center for research, training and service in the fields of disease control, biomedicine and public health. It comprises The Blair Research Laboratory (Established in 1939), Health Systems Research Unit (established in 1981) in Harare and the De Beers Research Laboratory (established in 1965) in Chiredzi. PMI supported entomological activities by providing training and updated staff at NIHR-Harare and De Beers Laboratory on insectary management and mosquito rearing to improve the insectaries and establish two colonies of susceptible mosquitoes for insecticide resistance monitoring. This included the refurbishment the Harare NIHR and Chiredzi insectaries, and improving the capacity of the entomology laboratories to carry out entomologic monitoring activities. PMI also provides reagents and supplies to NIHR-Harare to perform molecular and immunodiagnostic assays for the entomological monitoring activities.

*Progress during the last 12-18 months*

The two students in the first FETP cohort to receive PMI support both graduated the program in 2014 with merit and are currently employed by the MOHCC. PMI staff worked directly with the University of Zimbabwe FETP to enhance the malaria-focused education of supported fellows and others in the class, and provided guidance on modifying existing program documents to capture the malaria- and HIV/AIDS-focused projects and contributions. A PMI Resident Advisor participates in FETP conferences and acts as an attending or faculty member critiquing students' oral presentations. The FETP staff created a tool to capture the malaria-focused activities and contributions of PMI-supported residents. PMI-supported residents conducted at least three of six required projects on malaria topics.

*Plans and justification*

PMI will continue to support the FETP program in Zimbabwe to train talented epidemiologists. PMI and the NMCP will work with the FETP to identify areas to strengthen the malaria portion of the curriculum and provide increased malaria-specific training opportunities and projects for the students. PMI will build human capacity in malaria-related laboratory skills by partnering with a local university with a laboratory training program.

Many PMI activities result in strengthened health systems, even those that fall under other technical areas. Below, table 13 describes activities budgeted under all program areas that contribute to strengthening health systems in Zimbabwe, listed by health system building block.

*Proposed activities with FY 2016 funding: ($100,000)*

- *Support Field Epidemiology Training Program*: Promote malaria-specific field studies and support at least two trainees to enhance field epidemiology skills. The FETP funding is obligated to and managed by an implementing partner to provide support for the FETP activities in Zimbabwe. These funds will provide support for the execution of epidemiologic, outbreak investigation and surveillance evaluation-related activities in Zimbabwe involving the Zimbabwe FETP. This activity will strengthen mid- to high-level capacity, and develop skilled field supervisors in the malaria field as they learn how to actively identify, evaluate, and help scale up effective activities against malaria. *($100,000)*

**Table 13: Health Systems Strengthening Activities**

| HSS Building Block | Technical Area | Description of Activity |
|---|---|---|
| **Health Services** | Case Management | PMI will support the NMCP to conduct training and supportive supervision on malaria case management for primary health facility staff and VHWs on ACTs, RDTs, and MIP. Support will be provided for limited refresher training on case management and real time active case detection and follow-up in selected pre-elimination districts. |
| **Health Services** | Case Management | PMI will assess the status and needs of the VHW network and ability to support malaria control and pre-elimination activities to inform new project in following year. Support will be provided for training and supervision on malaria case management for VHWs at the community level on ACTs and RDTs. |
| **Health Workforce** | Health Systems Strengthening | The FETP will support malaria-specific field studies and at least two student trainees to enhance field epidemiology and malaria program management skills. |
| | Operations Research | PMI will analyze effectiveness of VHW networks to identify hotspots and respond to sporadic malaria transmission |
| **Health Information** | IRS | PMI will provide support to local institutions, including the NMCP and provincial level, for comprehensive entomological surveillance. |
| | Health Systems Strengthening | PMI will build laboratory capacity for both epidemiologic and entomologic surveillance sample analysis. |
| | M&E | PMI will provide technical and logistic support to the NMCP for malaria outbreak detection and response in outbreak-prone areas and/or pre-elimination settings. |
| | M&E | PMI will support quarterly district health team meetings, provincial M&E review meetings, training support and supervision across all levels. Recommendations from the assessment conducted with FY14 funds will be implemented. PMI will also continue to support the IDSR/DHIS2. |
| | M&E | PMI and the NMCP will utilize existing epidemiologic, entomologic and environmental data to produce map of malaria burden and risk. |
| **Essential Medical Products, Vaccines, and Technologies** | Insecticide-treated Nets | PMI will expand and strengthen routine ITN distribution systems in ANC, EPI, schools, and community. |
| **Health Finance** | NA | NA |
| **Leadership and Governance** | NA | NA |

## 6. Behavior change communication

*NMCP/PMI objectives*

The NMSP objectives form the basis for the implementation of the Behavior Change Communication (BCC) activities for the malaria control program in Zimbabwe. To achieve NMSP's desired outcome, PMI supports BCC activities that aim to promote correct and consistent use of ITNs, acceptance of IRS and adherence to diagnosis and treatment. PMI also supports BCC to improve uptake of IPTp in the areas where IPTp is used.

BCC activities are implemented at the national, provincial, district, and community levels. PMI support is approximately allocated to 15% national level and 85% at the community/ interpersonal level. Mobilizing traditional and religious community leaders and civic organizations to support and promote malaria prevention and control is critical for achievement of the NMCP's NMSP and PMI objectives.

At each primary health facility, there are one or more WHTs, which is composed of community health workers, school administrators, and community leaders who assist with malaria communication for IRS and LLIN distribution campaigns. Community malaria committees are made up of volunteers selected by their communities and trained by the primary health facility staff on key malaria messaging at an interpersonal communication level. With the implementation of community case management of malaria using VHWs, the NMCP emphasizes VHWs interactions with individuals, households, and small groups. The VHWs test, treat, and refer for malaria treatment as warranted and can serve as important conveyors of appropriate health messages and information.

*Progress since PMI was launched*

PMI has been supporting malaria BCC in Zimbabwe since the first MOP in 2011. This support included a revision of BCC materials and development and dissemination of new materials in the key malaria intervention areas (LLINs, IRS, MIP/IPTp, and Case Management). In 2012 PMI supported a small survey to gather data to better understand BCC needs in the malarious districts – both facilitators and barriers in different areas of the country. The MIS, conducted in March/April 2012, also provided additional useful information that has helped malaria partners better tailor BCC supporting messages to address critical gaps in knowledge, attitudes and practices.

In 2013, PMI supported the revision of the Zimbabwe Malaria Communication Strategy (2008-2013) and which was extended to 2017 in line with the NMSP. The strategy sets forth seven key interventions to be achieved; Vector Control (IRS, Larviciding and LLINs), Case Management,

Epidemic Preparedness and Response, IPTp, BCC, OR and M&E.

PMI also supported the development of a BCC Implementation Guide in 2014/15 which provides principles for malaria BCC including communication theories, situational analysis, strategic design (approach, messages, channels), development and testing of materials, implementation, and monitoring and evaluation. Malaria partners now use this reference guide to help with better planning and management of BCC activities to assist communities in malaria control.

Results from the 2013 PMI-supported TRaC survey shows that LLIN use increased from 37% in 2010 to 58% in 2013 (Figure 5). PMI partners followed-up on the TRaC results with BCC outreach to communities designed to increase LLIN use. BCC outreach also corresponded with additional LLIN campaigns in 2014 which NMCP estimates has pushed LLIN coverage levels to reach ~90% in malarious areas, achieving universal coverage. Data regarding progress on LLIN use and other malaria indicators is expected from the 2016 MIS results.

**Figure 5: Monitoring Individual Net Utilization, by Percent Surveyed, 2009-2013, Zimbabwe TRaC Survey**

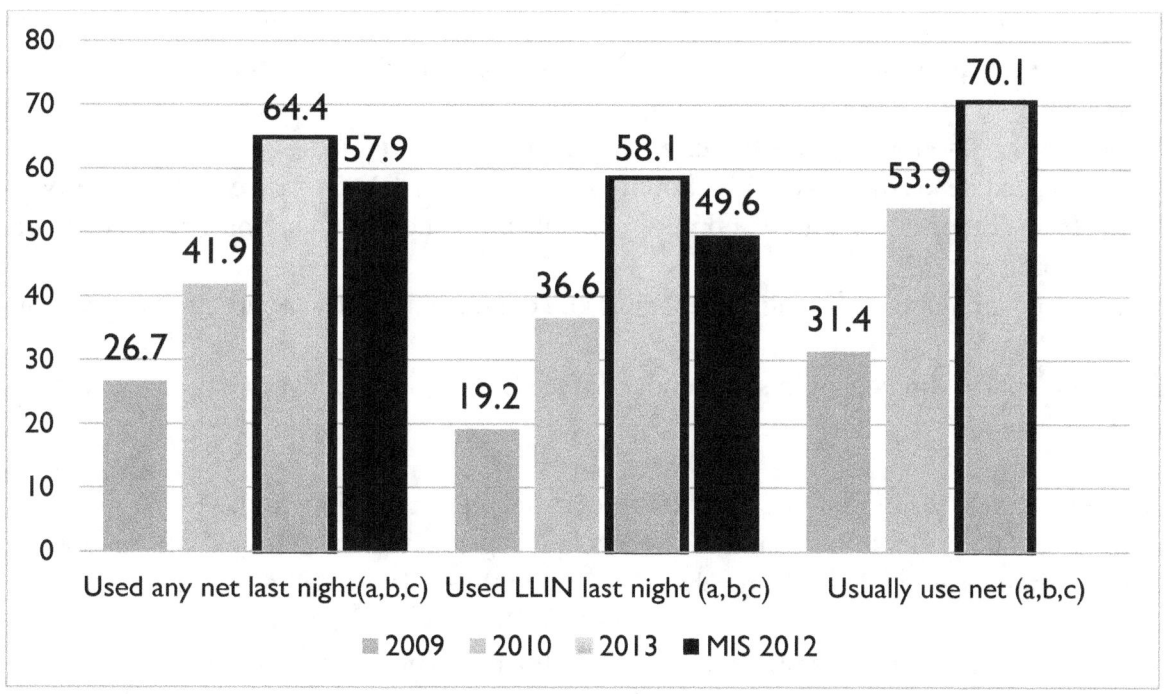

*Progress during the past 12 months*

This past year, PMI continued to work through VHWs to promote LLIN use and IPTp as well as early treatment seeking behavior. These outreach activities included routine and specific BCC activities in areas where outbreaks of malaria were reported. PMI also supported increased and broader dissemination of IRS spraying messaging to assist with information and acceptance on a new IRS chemical deployed in PMI-spraying areas, OPs. IRS messages prepare families for arrival of the sprayers and provide safety messages.

For LLIN activities in 2014-2015, PMI partners used a combination of outreach methods including radio, promotional materials, drama events (also known as road shows) and also added the branding of mini buses (known as *combi's* in Zimbabwe) and prominently located wall space at schools, clinics, and market places.

**Key LLIN Messages:**
1. LLINs are available for free in all malaria endemic areas.
2. Support and encouragement from family, friends, peers, and partner to use LLINs is valued.
3. LLINs are safe to use in malaria prevention.
4. Pregnant women and children under five years are more susceptible to malaria. Pregnant women have a compromised immunity due to pregnancy and children under five years do not have fully developed their immune system.
5. It is important to register and receive mosquito nets during the mass distribution exercise being carried out by the MOHCC.
6. People are urged to encourage each other to go and register for, as well as collect, their LLINs.
7. Mosquito nets should be properly hung, tucked in, and maintained.
8. Husbands and heads of households should assist and ensure that nets are hung properly. Mothers and other women in the home should ensure that children are properly tucked in before going to bed.
9. Sleeping under a treated mosquito net should be done consistently (every day) to prevent malaria.
10. Everyone in the family should sleep under a treated mosquito net every day to prevent malaria.

PMI supported a total of 133 radio messages on three radio stations nationwide, as well as producing over 24,000 promotional materials in two languages. Over one hundred road shows were performed in four target districts, reaching over 30,000 people.

PMI engaged schools to be malaria prevention and treatment advocates by supporting school health clubs and training 306 teachers as school health coordinators. Increasing malaria awareness among school cohorts ties into one of the routine distribution outlets that will soon be active in all elementary schools in malarious areas.

PMI partners engaged the NMCP and malaria partners in a workshop to identify an archetype to target for malaria messaging. The workshop assisted the NMCP to analyze the current situation, specify objectives for FY 2015, and identify strategies work plans and budgets.

**Figure 6: LLIN & IRS Facilitators and Barriers**

**LLIN Facilitators**
Perceived net efficacy
Perceived durability
Brand preference (nets over other mosquito killing/blocking methods)
Ensure good night sleep
Social support (family/friends view nets as good)
Social acceptability (similar to the above)
Malaria susceptibility
Malaria knowledge
Net attributes (nets are practical and easy to use)
Affordability (free)

**LLIN Barriers**
Bad habits
Discomfort during sleep (with nets -- perceived heat, breathing difficulty, restricted feeling, bad smells)
Adverse events
Seasonality of vectors
Inhibition of sex

**IRS Facilitators:**
Belief that IRS protects beyond the individual
Product efficacy
Possible dual outcome (kills other insects, bed bugs, cockroaches)

**IRS Barriers:**
Inconvenience
Use of similar alternative may be as effective (retail insect sprays)

Figure 6, shown above, lists facilitators and barriers identified during a recent partner assessment. The facilitators and barriers reveal important clues on what motivates people to use nets consistently and accept IRS willingly. The clues can be used to understand de-motivations as well. Malaria partners will develop BCC messages to encourage good behaviors based upon these findings. For example, findings show that people value a good night's sleep uninterrupted by annoying insects including mosquitoes that carry malaria. Therefore, messages can be formulated to extol this protective virtue of LLINs and remind people of this added value to motivate them to use LLINs. LLINs protect hard-working Zimbabweans from malaria and allow a peaceful, insect-free night's sleep. Similarly, an IRS barrier identified is the inconvenience of spraying day, for instance, having to move belongings out of the house and allow sprayers to come into the house, etc. Messages may be formulated to address this barrier by acknowledging it but assuring community members that the spraying team is there to assist in making spraying day as convenient as possible and reminding community members that a little inconvenience is worth it to protect you and your family from malaria -- a disease costly to your health and your pocket book.

PMI supported malaria commemoration events, including the Southern Africa Regional Community Malaria Day in January 2015, an event well attended by high-level political and malaria program leadership from throughout the Southern Africa region. In addition, PMI and partners also regularly supported the malaria BCC Working Group, an active technical group led by the NMCP, to share information, encourage high standards in BCC activities, and provide general guidance.

*Plans and justification*

PMI support will complement Global Fund malaria grant activities and, under the NMCP's guidance, focus on inter-personal communication, print materials development, pre-transmission season malaria prevention activities (LLINs, IRS), early careseeking behavior, and MIP uptake early in pregnancy. In line with the new NMCP Implementation Guidelines, PMI will use evidence-based messages, focusing on a target audience and delivery methods such as mass media, interpersonal communication, and print media.

In pre-elimination areas, PMI support for BCC will support active surveillance and case detection activities. Creating awareness and an understanding of pre-elimination is important, as is generating collective support for the ultimate goal of elimination. For example, BCC messages in pre-elimination districts will include information about reporting suspected malaria cases rapidly and following through with diagnosis, case confirmation, and treatment with primaquine quickly in order to limit further transmission. These messages will be targeted to health workers in facilities and village health workers in communities. Similar but differently tailored messages would be targeted to community members (with a less clinical focus). BCC messages can also help manage community expectations and encourage their participation in the urgent need to do malaria (and parasite) case follow-up testing within the radius of a discovered case. Taking case travel history is also an important part of case investigation in pre-elimination areas. BCC can help encourage communities to share this information and understand why it is important in understanding transmission.

PMI has planned a BCC assessment to take place in November 2015. The assessment will encompass a general review of what has been done in malaria BCC during the past three years at the national, provincial, district and community levels. Recommendations will include:

1. Next steps (programmatic, research, and managerial) for malaria BCC strategy implementation
2. Review of available funding (for implementation and capacity strengthening) and division of work amongst partners
3. How to improve BCC monitoring and evaluation at each level
4. Innovative BCC methods used elsewhere that could be applied and/or opportunities for learning from other countries

*Proposed activities with FY 2016 funding: ($400,000)*

*Support malaria BCC:* With FY 2016 funds PMI will support VHWs, school, and community leaders to conduct interpersonal communication on key malaria messages around LLINs, malaria in pregnancy, RDTs, and ACTs in the 47 districts with the highest malaria transmission. The school and community leaders' BCC activities will be complemented by printed materials that accompany packaged LLINs, RDTs and ACTs, radio spots, and drama skits at various locations including religious institutions, schools, and community events. The primary focus for all activities will be to support LLIN distribution (routine and campaign), improve MIP uptake (SP at each ANC at least one month apart, starting in the second trimester, use of LLINs during pregnancy, and early and effective diagnosis and treatment of malaria), and promote IRS and appropriate case management. The recommendations from the BCC assessment will provide information on improving PMI support in these primary focus areas. PMI will provide technical support for implementing the NMCP Communications Strategy Extension to 2017 in line with the NMSP. And, PMI will continue to support malaria advocacy and commemoration events and the BCC Working Group quarterly meetings *($400,000)*.

Specifically, the $400,000 budget for MOP16 can be disaggregated as follows:

a) Support LLIN distribution (routine and campaign) *($120,000)*
b) Improve MIP uptake (SP at each ANC at least one month apart, starting in the second trimester, use of LLINs during pregnancy, and early and effective diagnosis and treatment of malaria) *($100,000)*
c) Support BCC on appropriate case management *($150,000)*
d) Support for malaria advocacy and commemoration events and the BCC Working Group quarterly meetings *($30,000)*.

The proposed activities for FY16 may be considered for slight revision if the results from the BCC assessment in November 2015 indicate an immediate need to re-prioritize PMI-supported BCC activities.

## 7. Monitoring and evaluation

*NMCP/PMI objectives*

The NMCP's M&E Plan was released in 2009; a recent update was completed in 2014 to reflect the changing malaria landscape in Zimbabwe and align with the MSP and the WHO pre-elimination strategy. The M&E plan is based on the Global Fund M&E Toolkit, WHO recommended indicators, and internationally accepted tools and practices related to M&E. The plan defines national malaria indicators, sources and frequency of data collection, measurement procedures, and mechanisms to track progress towards targets. The main objective of the M&E plan is to provide a comprehensive tracking system that enables transparent and objective management of information on malaria control program activities for effective implementation of malaria interventions in Zimbabwe.

The M&E objectives are to:

- Ensure collection, collation, processing, analysis and use of malaria data at all levels of malaria control programming.
- Enable regular monitoring and documentation of program performance based on implementation plans and targets.
- Harmonize data collection based on standardized tools and indicators
- Establish and operationalize a comprehensive malaria database for warehousing, retrieving, and using malaria control information
- Facilitate and coordinate linkages of malaria control activities with other programs and partners in order to eliminate duplication
- Provide information for evidence-based decision making at all levels.

Surveillance, M&E, and research in malaria have evolved over time and have helped improve the quality of the malaria data in the HMIS reporting morbidity and mortality data from each district. Major M&E activities include nationwide surveys (2015 ZDHS and an MIS in 2016), program reviews, planning and data review meetings, supervisory visits to provincial and district health offices, collaboration with global and national institutions, strengthening routine data collection and management, and outbreak investigations and response. Information obtained is used for evidence-based decision making, program management, and accountability.

*Progress since PMI was launched*

Surveillance, M&E, and operational research data are collected, reported, and recorded from many channels including routine data systems, programmatic monitoring, and national surveys. Additional M&E data are available, including insecticide resistance monitoring, vector mapping, and therapeutic efficacy studies. These data will be used to develop an in-depth and up to date map of malaria burden and risk to inform future programmatic decisions. The table below summarizes some of the key M&E data for malaria in Zimbabwe, including national-level surveys, routine and specialized surveillance systems, and other data sources.

**Table 14: Key Monitoring & Evaluation Data Sources, 2009-2018, Zimbabwe**

| Data Source | Survey Activities | Calendar Year | | | | | | | | | |
|---|---|---|---|---|---|---|---|---|---|---|---|
| | | 2009 | 2010 | 2011 | 2012 | 2013 | 2014 | 2015 | 2016 | 2017 | 201 |
| Household surveys | Demographic Health Survey (DHS)* | | X | | | | | X | | | |
| | AIDS Indicator Survey (AIS)* | | | | | | | X | | | |
| | Malaria Indicator Survey (MIS) | | | | X | | | | X | | |
| | Multiple Indicator Monitoring Survey (MIMS)* | X | | | | | X | | | | |
| | EPI survey* | | | | | X | | | | | |
| Health facility and other surveys | Rapid Impact Assessment* | | | | | X | | | | | |
| | Tracking Results Continuously (TRaC)* | X | | X | | X^ | | | | | |
| | EUV survey | | | | X | X | X | X | X | | |
| | LLIN durability monitoring | | | | | | | X | X | | |
| Malaria surveillance and routine system support | Support to malaria surveillance system | | | | X | X | X | X* | X* | X* | X* |
| | Support to HMIS/IDSR | | | | X | X | X | X | X | X | X |
| Therapeutic | In vivo drug efficacy testing | | | | | X** | X** | | | X** | |
| Entomology | Entomological surveillance and resistance monitoring | | | | | X | X | X | X | X | X |

Footnote: *Not PMI funded ^Partially PMI supported **WHO supported/will support two additional sites

*Routine data systems*

The main sources of routine malaria data that form the foundation for the country's HMIS are the District Health information System 2 (DHIS2), a web-based HMIS reporting system, and the Rapid Disease Notification System (RDNS). Zimbabwe transitioned to DHIS2 nationally in January 2014. Monthly reports on malaria cases and deaths from all public health facilities and mission clinics are reported through the DHIS2 platform. The reported malaria-related data includes the number of suspected cases, proportion of suspected malaria cases that received parasitological test (microscopy/RDT), number of parasitologically-confirmed cases, ACT consumption, and IPTp uptake. Ongoing M&E and data quality assurance to maintain the system as a reliable source of health facility data includes on-site validation checks, supervision and supervisory visits, training new staff to fill vacancies, frequent re-trainings at the district and provincial levels, and ensuring internet connectivity. At each data source point (clinic, rural health center, hospital, IRS camp site) there is a person responsible for reviewing all data generated to ensure good data quality before sending to the next level which in most cases is the district level. Data validation is also conducted at district level before it goes to the provincial level where the data is also validated before they are sent to national level. The same process takes place at national level before the data is widely shared outside MOHCC structures. Special site visits are conducted by M&E specialist from MOHCC and partners (such as USAID, Global Fund and implementing partners) to assess data quality, collection and management procedures. A checklist is usually used that focuses on reliability, validity, timeliness, integrity, and precision. As data are being reviewed, feedback and mentoring is provided to help all those involved at various levels. The national reporting system is considered to be high quality, timely, and complete; during the most recent reporting in 2014, reporting completeness was approximately 98% of 1,700 facilities reporting and timeliness was 67.5%.

The RDNS provides weekly data on 12 epidemic-prone diseases, including laboratory-confirmed malaria cases and deaths, from approximately 1,500 health facilities nationwide. Health facilities reporting to RDNS submit data to the districts which then transmit to provincial and central levels. A weekly report is produced and distributed to the national program areas.

In 2014, 34% of cases were associated with 130 outbreaks, mainly occurring in two of these border provinces, Manicaland and Mashonaland East. "Outbreaks" in Zimbabwe are defined by the number of cases exceeding the health facility weekly expected case count, or threshold value. Malaria epidemic thresholds are calculated using weekly data. An alert epidemic threshold is reached when the number of confirmed weekly cases exceeds the three-year mean of the confirmed weekly cases plus one standard deviation. An action epidemic threshold is reached when the reported weekly cases exceed the three-year mean plus two standard deviations of reported cases. A priority of the NMCP is to continue improving outbreak detection and improve support for response. The NMCP, with support from PMI, will continue to ensure threshold values are being calculated correctly and evaluate how the threshold values are identifying outbreaks compared with moderate seasonal malaria increases. Barriers for rapid detection and response include facilities not having any or not current thresholds calculated, limited evidence of data use where health facility staff not trained on utilizing the thresholds in order to recognize and report an increase in cases in a timely manner, and the lack of district, provincial, or national staff to have the flexibility to provide commodities or control measures quickly to respond to identified outbreaks.

*Programmatic monitoring*

Programmatic data on IRS, LLIN distribution, and entomologic monitoring are managed by the NMCP and are used to monitor and report on the implementation of all malaria control activities. Data are collected from the sub-district level and passed through district and provincial levels to the national level on a weekly, monthly, or quarterly basis, depending on the data being reported; however, a standardized entomologic monitoring database does not yet exist and should be developed as soon as possible.

*LLIN durability monitoring*

The WHO Pesticide Evaluation Scheme (WHOPES) recommends that all LLIN programs monitor different net products in their local settings. However, following the mass LLIN distribution campaign in 2014, prospective LLIN durability monitoring was not conducted, as the study could not be initiated within 12 months after the campaign.

*National surveys*

In April 2009, UNICEF supported a MIMS, which is similar to the Multiple Indicator Cluster Survey and included a malaria module. The most recent DHS was completed in 2010-11 and also included a standardized malaria module. Data from the DHS and MIMS provided pre-PMI baseline estimates for most of the coverage indicators used by PMI. In 2012, PMI supported an MIS, which also included anemia and parasitemia biomarkers collected from children aged 6-59 months in households from 51 malaria endemic districts in 8 rural provinces. Key results from the 2012 MIS include the finding of low national parasitemia in children less than five years of age: 1% by RDT confirmation and 0.4% by microscopy confirmation, yet there was high anemia prevalence. Additional findings from the survey include: moderate ITN utilization, low IPTp uptake, and that radio or TV were not common sources of malaria information. The next DHS will be conducted mid-year 2015, but will not be measuring parasitemia. High-quality district-level malaria data are needed by the NMCP for planning purposes, therefore a second MIS will be conducted in 2016, which will be four years after the 2012 MIS. The PMI team is working closely with the survey partners and stakeholders to determine the optimal strategy for collecting the necessary biomarkers.

Ten EUV surveys (a quarterly survey to verify availability of malaria commodities in health facilities and warehouses), were conducted in 2012 through 2015. Quarterly reports are provided summarizing the EUV activities and findings. These reports provide key observations, recommendations, and next steps for commodity distribution and are distributed widely to MOHCC personnel and in-country partners in Zimbabwe. To improve the utility of the EUV in Zimbabwe for 2016 and onward, the survey tool, as well as the timing and facilities visited during the survey, will be adjusted to better accommodate the seasonality and epidemiology of malaria in the country.

*Progress during the last 12-18 months*

In addition to the surveys conducted as mentioned above, a national MCCM standard training package developed for health care worker trainings, including VHW trainings, was finalized in 2014 and 3,000 copies were printed. As part of the iCCM support for VHWs, a supportive supervision system with a peer-centered supervision model was successfully implemented in 1 district in Manicaland with 40 supervisors oriented. Trainings are ongoing; in 2014 a total of 1,464 village health workers, 47 VHW trainers or supervisors, 196 nurse aides, and 127 school health coordinators were trained on MCCM. PMI supported two district health team meetings in Chipinge and Mutare with a total of 169 participants, 5 M&E trainings of 196 participants, and 1 IDSR training, which included 40 participants. Zimbabwe and Mozambique cross-border activities to evaluate drivers of malaria and health care seeking behaviors along the border were initiated.

PMI supported Zimbabwe MOHCC to conduct quarterly EUV exercises for malaria commodities (medications and RDTs). The EUV assesses the availability of malaria commodities at facility level, identifies areas of strength and weakness in the supply chain and malaria case management, and provides data and insight for analysis, advocacy, and decision-making on a quarterly basis.

Through PMI support a robust entomological monitoring was completed, as part of monitoring of its indoor residual spraying (IRS) program in Manicaland Province. Insecticide resistance to the insecticide being used at the time in Manicaland Province was identified, thereby resulting in a change of insecticides to organophosphates in four districts in Manicaland. PMI supported additional entomologic monitoring in other provinces as well, which was used by the NMCP to validate the residual efficacy of insecticides used during the IRS campaigns, gain data on insecticide resistance and vector behavior, and provide further entomological data for the NMCP to consider for future IRS campaign planning.

*Plans and justification*

PMI will continue work with the NMCP to support monitoring the quality of malaria data collected through the HMIS to ensure that the programmatic needs of the NMCP are met. The need to use real-time data to identify temporal and geographic variations in morbidity or mortality in pre-elimination and outbreak-prone settings such as Zimbabwe is a high priority to ensure the success of the program. With FY 2016 funding, PMI will continue to support malaria surveillance, monitoring and evaluation activities and support enhancing outbreak detection and response. PMI will work with the NMCP to find ways to balance prevention and control activities in high burden areas with successfully implementing pre-elimination activities at the community level in low burden areas. PMI will support outbreak response activities in no more than two provinces, including providing technical assistance to the NMCP and health facility staff to quickly and properly identify outbreaks, develop response plans, and provide corrective measures such as sending staff from the district, province, or national level and/or additional commodities, as needed. PMI will continue support for M&E trainings at all levels including village and community health workers as well as supervisory and district health facility trainings. In addition, PMI support will be used to facilitate quarterly meetings for district-, provincial-, national-level, and cross-border representatives to meet and discuss surveillance and M&E related issues.

PMI will support the LLIN durability monitoring of LLINs that were distributed in a large-scale school-based distribution in 2015. PMI will prospectively monitor LLIN durability from a cohort of LLINs distributed during a large-scale school distribution campaign in 2015 at 6, 12, 24, and 36 months post-distribution to determine the LLIN performance under Zimbabwe field conditions, the findings of which will be used to guide the country-specific LLIN replacement rate. The data can also be used to refine communications efforts designed to improve the care of nets within households.

*Proposed activities with FY 2016 funding: ($710,000)*

- *End-use verification survey:* Conduct quarterly surveys to assess availability of malaria commodities in health facilities and warehouses. *($100,000)*

- *Outbreak investigation and response:* Provide technical and logistic support to the NMCP for malaria outbreak detection and response in outbreak-prone areas and/or pre-elimination settings. PMI will support training to improve capacity to analyze and monitor the malaria trends, and improve preparedness for epidemic detection and response. *($100,000)*

- *Conduct LLIN durability monitoring:* Continue prospective monitoring of the performance and durability of LLINs distributed during a large-scale school-based distribution in 2015. This will be the 12- and 24-month post-distribution assessments. *($100,000)*

- *National M&E support:* Support quarterly district health team meetings and conduct training support to epidemic prone districts to ensure early outbreak detection and effective response. Implement recommendations from the training needs assessment conducted with FY 2014 funds. *($300,000)*

- *Malaria burden and risk stratification mapping*: Support the development of a malaria burden and risk map utilizing existing epidemiologic, entomologic, and environmental data. *($100,000)*

- *Technical assistance:* One CDC TDY to support PMI Zimbabwe M&E activities. *($10,000)*

## 8. Operational research

*NMCP/PMI objectives*

As one of the newer PMI countries, Zimbabwe is still early in the development of an operational research (OR) portfolio. However, NMCP has identified some priority areas for research, they include: 1) malaria in mobile and remote populations; 2) role of community health workers in malaria pre-elimination; and 3) documenting progress towards pre-elimination.

*Progress during the past 12-18 months*

In October 2014, a concept note was submitted to the OR Working Group for consideration to determine the optimal diagnostic measurement of malaria burden in a low transmission setting during the 2016 Zimbabwe Malaria Indicator Survey. This study will evaluate microscopy, rapid diagnostic tests, and serologic and polymerase chain reaction analysis of dried blood spots collected during the national household survey. Approval by the PMI OR committee is pending.

The findings of this OR activity will inform future national household surveys in Zimbabwe and other PMI countries that are considering using these additional tests.

**Table 15: Operational Research Studies**

| Completed OR Studies | | | |
|---|---|---|---|
| **Title** | **Start date** | **End date** | **Budget** |
| None | | | |
| **Ongoing OR Studies** | **Start date (est.)** | **End date (est.)** | **Budget** |
| Title: *An evaluation of microscopy, rapid diagnostic tests, and serologic and polymerase chain reaction analysis of dried blood spots from the 2016 Zimbabwe Malaria Indicator Survey* | 06/2016 | 06/2017 | $100,000 plus PMI OR Core Funds |
| **Planned OR Studies FY 2016** | **Start date (est.)** | **End date (est.)** | **Budget** |
| Title: Assessing the effectiveness of VHWs in decreasing the malaria morbidity and mortality burden through active or reactive case detection in hotspot and/or pre-elimination areas in Zimbabwe | 10/2016 | 06/2017 | $233,323 |
| Title: *Assessing the potential for and human risk factors associated with outdoor feeding by malaria vectors in Manicaland Province* | 10/2016 | 06/2017 | $150,000 |

*Plans and justification*

**Assessing the effectiveness of VHWs in decreasing the malaria morbidity and mortality burden through active or reactive case detection in hotspot and/or pre-elimination areas in Zimbabwe**

As malaria transmission declines, control or pre-elimination efforts can be hindered by persistent areas of transmission, or hotspots. Strategies for addressing these focal areas of transmission include active and reactive case detection and mass drug administration of an effective malaria treatment to an entire population. In Zimbabwe, VHWs provide iCCM services in communities, including malaria community case management. It is feasible that VHWs could be utilized in deploying certain mentioned strategies to further reduce malaria transmission in identified hotspot or pre-elimination areas; however, their effectiveness needs to be evaluated in the Zimbabwe context.

*Objectives*
1. To evaluate the effectiveness of VHWs in decreasing the malaria morbidity and mortality burden through active or reactive case detection.
2. To determine the potential for VHWs to conduct mass-drug administration of DHA-PQ in a community or area identified as a hotspot for malaria transmission

**Assessing the potential for and human risk factors associated with outdoor feeding by malaria vectors in Manicaland Province**

Insecticide-treated mosquito nets and IRS are the two primary vector-control interventions used for large-scale malaria prevention and are an integral component of Zimbabwe's national malaria control strategy. Between 2010 and 2014, with support from the Global Fund and PMI, the NMCP distributed 6 million LLINs in 37 districts with highest burden of malaria through universal mass campaigns and has carried out IRS in targeted malaria endemic districts across Zimbabwe. Despite the high coverage of vector-control activities, malaria prevalence in Manicaland Province remains high as compared to some other provinces in Zimbabwe.

One factor that might help explain the persistence of malaria in Manicaland is that ITNs and IRS primarily address endophagic (indoor feeding) and endophilic (indoor resting) vectors. The presence of exophagic (outdoor feeding) and exophilic (outdoor resting) mosquitoes may limit their effectiveness. The impact of IRS and ITNs on outdoor-biting vectors and therefore the protection of people during outdoor nighttime activities, including outdoor sleeping is unclear and represents a key challenge for the effectiveness of these vector-control activities. No systematic study has been conducted to confirm if spending time outdoors at night is a risk factor for malaria in Zimbabwe. The proposed study will be conducted in Manicaland an area marked by seasonal malaria transmission with severe outbreaks occurring during the wet season. A recent research by the International Centers of Excellence in Malaria Research (ICEMR) that began in 2012 to assess malaria burden in the region collected mosquito samples during the wet seasons of 2012-2014 using CDC light traps and pyrethroid spray catches. Morphological identification indicated that the predominant malaria vector is *Anopheles funestus senso lato*. Molecular identification of samples from the 2012-2013 collections also confirmed these results, with samples being *An. funestus senso stricto* or *Anopheles leesoni*, both members of the *An. funestus* species complex. Blood meal analysis indicated that these mosquitoes feed predominantly on human populations. The study did not include assessment of outdoor biting. Recent studies in Benin and Tanzania have reported significant changes in the host-seeking behavior of the *A. funestus* population after scaling up universal coverage of LLINs. Results showed that three years after implementation of LLIN at community level, *A. funestus* bit later during the night (almost at dawn) and more frequently outdoors, compared with the baseline survey. Findings from similar study in Tanzania showed a shift from indoor to outdoor biting in relation to increasing coverage of pyrethroid-impregnated nets (Moiroux N. et al and Russell TL et al).[1] The hypothesis in the proposed OR activity is that with the increased LLINs coverage, as well as IRS spraying in Manicaland, the risk of malaria is likely to be associated with outdoor human-vector contact. Study findings will inform the design of behavior change communication or other interventions to reduce the risk of malaria infection during outdoor activities.

*Objective*
1. To examine the presence of outdoor feeding malaria vectors and assess human nighttime activities, including outdoor-sleeping, that might increase exposure to malaria infection.

*Proposed activities with FY 2016 funding: ($393,323)*

- *Operational research study:* Assessing the effectiveness of VHWs in decreasing the malaria morbidity and mortality burden through active or reactive case detection in hotspot and/or pre-elimination areas in Zimbabwe. *($233,323)*

- *Operational research study:* Assessing the potential for and human risk factors associated with outdoor feeding by malaria vectors in Manicaland Province. *($150,000)*

- *Technical assistance:* One CDC TDY to support PMI Zimbabwe's OR activities. *($10,000)*

## 9. Staffing and administration

Two health professionals serve as resident advisors to oversee PMI in Zimbabwe, one representing CDC and one representing USAID. In addition, one or more Foreign Service Nationals (FSNs) work as part of the PMI team. All PMI staff members are part of a single interagency team led by the USAID Mission Director or his/her designee in country. The PMI team shares responsibility for development and implementation of PMI strategies and work plans, coordination with national authorities, managing collaborating agencies and supervising day-to-day activities. Candidates for resident advisor positions (whether initial hires or replacements) will be evaluated and/or interviewed jointly by USAID and CDC, and both agencies will be involved in hiring decisions, with the final decision made by the individual agency.

The PMI professional staff work together to oversee all technical and administrative aspects of PMI, including finalizing details of the project design, implementing malaria prevention and treatment activities, monitoring and evaluation of outcomes and impact, reporting of results, and providing guidance to PMI partners.

---

[1] Nicolas Moiroux, Marinely B. Gomez, Cédric Pennetier, Emmanuel Elanga, Armel Djènontin, Fabrice Chandre, Innocent Djègbé, Hélène Guis, and Vincent Corbel :Changes in Anopheles funestus Biting Behavior Following Universal Coverage of Long-Lasting Insecticidal Nets in Benin: The Journal of Infectious Disease 2012 206: 1622-1629.

The PMI lead in country is the USAID Mission Director. The day-to-day lead for PMI is delegated to the USAID Health Office Director and thus the two PMI resident advisors, one from USAID and one from CDC, report to the USAID Health Office Director for day-to-day leadership, and work together as a part of a single interagency team. The technical expertise housed in Atlanta and Washington guides PMI programmatic efforts.

The two PMI resident advisors are based within the USAID health office and are expected to spend approximately half their time sitting with and providing technical assistance to the national malaria control programs and partners.

Locally-hired staff to support PMI activities either in Ministries or in USAID will be approved by the USAID Mission Director. Because of the need to adhere to specific country policies and USAID accounting regulations, any transfer of PMI funds directly to Ministries or host governments will need to be approved by the USAID Mission Director and Controller, in addition to the US Global Malaria Coordinator.

*Proposed activities with FY 2016 funding: ($1,450,000)*

- *USAID in country staffing and administration ($900,000)*

- *CDC in-country staffing and administration ($550,000)*

## Table 1: Budget Breakdown by Mechanism

## President's Malaria Initiative – ZIMBABWE

## Planned Malaria Obligations for FY 2016

| Mechanism | Geographic Area | Activity | Budget ($) | % |
|---|---|---|---|---|
| TBD – Supply Chain Contract | National | Procure ITNs, ACTs, RDTs, and other commodities. Provide technical assistance to supply chain management | $4,746,677 | 33% |
| ZAPIM | National | Support for routine ITN distribution; technical assistance for supportive supervision of health workers and village health workers; capacity building for local laboratories and BCC messages. Support for M&E activities. | $3,083,323 | 21% |
| AIRS 2 TO 6 | National | IRS implementation; entomological monitoring. | $4,900,000 | 34% |
| CDC/IAA | National | Technical assistance, supplies and administration | $720,000 | 5% |
| VectorWorks | 4 IRS districts | Assessment on needs and strategies for special populations | $150,000 | 1% |
| USAID in country staffing and administration | National | Support for USAID staffing and administration costs | $900,000 | 6% |
| Total | | | $14,500,000 | 100% |

**Table 2: Budget Breakdown by Activity**

**President's Malaria Initiative – ZIMBABWE**

**Planned Malaria Obligations for FY 2016**

| Proposed Activity | Mechanism | Budget | | Geographic Area | Description |
|---|---|---|---|---|---|
| | | Total $ | Commodity $ | | |
| **PREVENTIVE ACTIVITIES** | | | | | |
| **Insecticide-treated Nets** | | | | | |
| Procurement of ITNs | TBD – Supply Chain Contract | $1,600,000 | $1,600,000 | Nationwide | 310,680 LLINs |
| Distribution of ITNs | ZAPIM | $500,000 | - | Nationwide | Support for routine distribution, expanding routine distribution network from pilot to full implementation in malarious areas |
| **SUBTOTAL ITNs** | | **$2,100,000** | **$1,600,000** | | |
| **Indoor Residual Spraying** | | | | | |

76

| Activity | Mechanism | | | Coverage | Notes |
|---|---|---|---|---|---|
| Support IRS activities | AIRS 2 TO 6 | $4,500,000 | $1,500,000 | High burden malaria districts (Likely Manicaland and/or Mashonaland East, Mashonaland Central Provinces) | Selection of PMI-supported spraying areas has recently been the districts with the highest burden (in Manicaland) but final selection of PMI-supported districts will depend on 2015 malaria epidemiology and entomological data |
| Entomological surveillance and monitoring | AIRS 2 TO 6 | $400,000 | - | 16 sentinel sites plus limited urban sites | provide support to local institutions for comprehensive entomological surveillance |
| Entomologic supplies | CDC/IAA | $11,000 | $11,000 | Nationwide | procure laboratory supplies necessary for entomological surveillance |
| TA for entomological surveillance | CDC/IAA | $29,000 | - | Nationwide | Two CDC TDYs to provide support for entomological activities. |
| **SUBTOTAL IRS** | | **$4,940,000** | **$1,511,000** | | |
| **Malaria in Pregnancy** | | | | | |
| Procurement of SP | TBD – Supply Chain Contract | $33,919 | $33,919 | 30 IPTp districts | Purchase approximately 161,000 treatments of SP for IPTp |

| Support health worker training and supervision in MIP prevention and management | ZAPIM | See case management section | - | Nationwide | Training and supportive supervision in MIP prevention and management |
|---|---|---|---|---|---|
| Support for MIP BCC activities | ZAPMI | See behavior change communication section | - | Nationwide | Focus on community sensitization, improved IPTp uptake, and other preventive measures such as the use of LLINs during pregnancy |
| Subtotal Malaria in Pregnancy | | $33,919 | $33,919 | | |
| **SUBTOTAL PREVENTIVE** | | **$7,073,919** | **$3,144,919** | | |

**CASE MANAGEMENT**

**Diagnosis and Treatment**

| Procurement of RDTs | TBD – Supply Chain Contract | $1,000,000 | $1,000,000 | Nationwide | Purchase approximately 1,886,792 million RDTs for use at primary health facilities and by VHWs. Assume $ .53 per RDT. |
|---|---|---|---|---|---|

| Activity | Source | Amount | Amount | Location | Description |
|---|---|---|---|---|---|
| Procurement of ACTs | TBD – Supply Chain Contract | $594,000 | $594,000 | Nationwide | 517,883 total ACT courses of treatment at an average cost of $1.21 per treatment. This assumes 497,667 AL and 20,216 ASAQ courses of treatment. |
| Procurement of injectable artesunate for treatment of severe malaria | TBD – Supply Chain Contract | $431,930 | $431,930 | Nationwide | Severe cases seen at or referred to hospitals and health facilities. Assume 5% presenting cases (60% pediatric, 40% adult) plus 5% uncomplicated becoming severe. 166,000 vials at $2.60 per vial. |
| Procurement of artesunate suppositories | TBD – Supply Chain Contract | $36,828 | $36,828 | Nationwide | To be used by VHWs pre-referral to a health facility. 200mg and 50mg doses, 29,700 each at an average cost of $0.60 per suppository. |
| Procure malaria diagnostic supplies | TBD – Supply Chain Contract | $50,000 | $50,000 | Nationwide | Purchase laboratory supplies and reagents to support microscopy diagnosis of malaria. |
| Technical assistance trip to support diagnostics | CDC/IAA | $10,000 | - | Nationwide | One CDC TDY to support on-going diagnostic activities in country. |

79

| Activity | | Location | | | Description |
|---|---|---|---|---|---|
| Facilitate supportive supervision of malaria case management for health facility workers | ZAPIM | Nationwide | $500,000 | - | Support NMCP to conduct supportive supervision on malaria case management for primary health facility staff on ACTs, RDTs, and MIP. Support for limited refresher training on case management. Support real time active case detection and follow-up in selected pre-elimination districts. |
| Assessment, training and supervision of VHWs | ZAPIM | Nationwide | $500,000 | - | Assessment of status and needs of VHW network and ability to support malaria control and pre-elimination activities to inform new project in following year. Support training and supervision on malaria case management for VHWs at the community level on ACTs and RDTs. |
| Meet service gaps for mobile populations | ZAPIM | Eastern border provinces | $200,000 | - | Address previously identified gaps in protection and treatment for mobile populations. |
| Strengthen malaria diagnostic capacity | ZAPIM | Nationwide | $150,000 | - | Provide support for building laboratory capacity in collaboration with national partners |
| **Subtotal Diagnosis and Treatment** | | | **$3,472,758** | **$2,112,758** | |

**Pharmaceutical Management**

| Category | Implementer | Location | | | Description |
|---|---|---|---|---|---|
| Supply chain strengthening | TBD – Supply Chain Contract | Nationwide | $900,000 | - | Support ZIPS/ZAPS, including operational costs, technical assistance, trainings, quantification support and logistics. |
| Subtotal Pharmaceutical Management | | | $900,000 | - | |
| **SUBTOTAL CASE MANAGEMENT** | | | **$4,372,758** | **$2,112,758** | |
| **HEALTH SYSTEM STRENGTHENING / CAPACITY BUILDING** | | | | | |
| FETP | CDC/IAA (AFENET) | Nationwide | $100,000 | - | Support malaria-specific field studies and at least two student trainees to enhance field epidemiology skills. |
| **SUBTOTAL HSS & CAPACITY BUILDING** | | | **$100,000** | - | |
| **BEHAVIOR CHANGE COMMUNICATION** | | | | | |
| Support malaria BCC | ZAPIM | Nationwide | $400,000 | - | Support malaria BCC for LLINs, MIP, IRS, and case management, particularly for the VHWs. Adapt/ develop appropriate materials for mobile and border populations. |

| | | | $400,000 | $0 | |
|---|---|---|---|---|---|
| **SUBTOTAL BCC** | | | | | |
| **MONITORING AND EVALUATION** | | | | | |
| End-use verification | TBD – Supply Chain Contract | | $100,000 | - | Nationwide | Quarterly surveys to assess availability of malaria commodities in health facilities and warehouses. |
| Outbreak investigation and response | ZAPIM | | $100,000 | - | Outbreak-prone areas | Technical and logistic support to the NMCP for malaria outbreak detection and response in outbreak-prone areas and/or pre-elimination settings |
| Conduct LLINs durability monitoring | ZAPIM | | $100,000 | - | Nationwide | Third year follow-up LLIN durability monitoring for LLINs distributed through school-based distribution campaign |
| Support & facilitate M&E activities, including IDSR/DHIS2 at provincial, district and primary health facility levels | ZAPIM | | $300,000 | - | Nationwide | Support quarterly district health team meetings, provincial M&E review meetings, training support and supervision across all levels. Implement recommendations from assessment conducted with FY14 funds. Funds will also continue to support the IDSR/DHIS2. |

| Activity | Partner | Location | | | Notes |
|---|---|---|---|---|---|
| Malaria burden and risk stratification mapping | ZAPIM | Nationwide | $100,000 | - | Utilize existing epidemiologic, entomologic and environmental data to produce map of malaria burden and risk |
| Technical assistance trip to support M&E | CDC/IAA | Nationwide | $10,000 | - | One CDC TDY to support on-going M&E activities in country |
| **SUBTOTAL M&E** | | | **$710,000** | **$0** | |
| **OPERATIONS RESEARCH** | | | | | |
| Analyze effectiveness of VHW networks to identify hotspots and respond to sporadic malaria transmission | ZAPIM | Hotspot transmission areas | $233,323 | - | |
| Analyze sleeping habits/ behavior and links to malaria transmission | VectorWorks | 4 PMI IRS districts | $150,000 | - | Focus on identifying and addressing difficult-to-reach special populations (occupations that often don't get included in normal quantifications) |

| | | | | | |
|---|---|---|---|---|---|
| Technical Assistance | CDC | $10,000 | | | One CDC TDY to support PMI Zimbabwe's OR activities |
| **SUBTOTAL OR** | | **$393,323** | $0 | | |
| **IN-COUNTRY STAFFING AND ADMINISTRATION** | | | | | |
| In country staffing and administration costs | USAID | $900,000 | - | Nationwide | Support for USAID staffing and administration costs |
| In country staffing and administration costs | CDC | $550,000 | - | Nationwide | Support for CDC staffing and administration costs |
| **SUBTOTAL IN-COUNTRY STAFFING** | | **$1,450,000** | - | | |
| **GRAND TOTAL** | | **$14,500,000** | **$5,257,677** | | |